ADVANCE PRAISE FOR *WINNING THE CUSTOMER*

Winning the Customer is a must-read for anyone interested in sports marketing because it is chock full of examples on how to deliver more value to sponsors and generate more revenue for sports properties. Lou's book is an invaluable tool for those who want to stay ahead of the game in this highly competitive industry.

—MICHAEL OZANIAN
Executive Editor, *Forbes Sports Money*

Lou's down-to-earth stories are enjoyable to read while capturing insightful methods to build relationships that generate revenue. Many of the anecdotes are from the sports business, but the philosophies apply to any industry.

—GEORGE PYNE
President, IMG Sports & Entertainment

The principals and disciplines in *Winning the Customer* are perfect for turning your customers into fans. Lou is such a great storyteller that he makes a pure business book a very enjoyable read.

—KAREN KAPLAN
President, Hill Holliday

From small corner store to a huge global conglomerate, *Winning the Customer* captures the essence of what marketing is all about. The experience Lou has gained throughout his career is revealed in this real-life philosophy on how to build relationships and profits. This marketing manifesto is applicable in any worldwide industry.

—JOHN BERYLSON
Chairman, Millwall F.C.

Winning the Customer drives home valuable insights into today's marketing successes: customer focus, relationship marketing, and teamwork. All based on insights gleaned from Lou's spectacularly rich set of experiences.

—MATT RYAN
President, Global Brands, Chairman, Euro RSCG New York

A roadmap for success in the field of marketing. Whether you are a long-time veteran marketer or a rookie in the field, it doesn't matter. Lou Imbriano shares with you his time-tested, proven methods that manifest proven results. All you need to do is take the nuggets of golden wisdom he so generously shares in this book, and apply them to your business.

—BOB BURG
Coauthor of *The Go-Giver* and Author of *Endless Referrals*

WINNING

— THE —

CUSTOMER

WINNING

== THE ==

CUSTOMER

TURN CONSUMERS INTO FANS
AND GET THEM TO
SPEND MORE

LOU IMBRIANO
ELIZABETH KING

New York   Chicago   San Francisco   Lisbon   London
Madrid   Mexico City   Milan   New Delhi
San Juan   Seoul   Singapore
Sydney   Toronto

The **McGraw·Hill** Companies

2 3 4 5 6 7 QVS/QVS 20 19 18 17 16

ISBN: 978-0-07-177526-7
MHID: 0-07-177526-9

e-ISBN: 978-0-07-177529-8
e-MHID: 0-07-177529-3

This publication is designed to provide accurate and authoritative information in regard to the subject matter covered. It is sold with the understanding that neither the authors nor the publisher is engaged in rendering legal, accounting, securities trading, or other professional service. If legal advice or other expert assistance is required, the services of a competent professional person should be sought.

—From a Declaration of Principles Jointly Adopted by a Committee of the American Bar Association and a Committee of Publishers and Associations

McGraw-Hill books are available at special quantity discounts to use as premiums and sales promotions or for use in corporate training programs. To contact a representative, please e-mail us at bulksales@mcgraw-hill.com.

This book is printed on acid-free paper.

To my family: You all have contributed to
this book and everything I do.

—*Lou*

This one is for Amy B.

—*Elizabeth*

There are so many people to thank, and I am sorry if I missed anyone. Please chalk it up to a rookie mistake. I have to start off by thanking my wife, Patricia: P, you are a consistent source of love and dedication and have been with me since I made five dollars an hour. Your support has gotten me through a lot and given me the confidence to push on. Oh, thanks for being a great proofreader, too. We also have great kids who understood that when daddy had his headphones on, that meant he was writing, and they shouldn't jump on him and distract him. I love you, V and A.

Thank you also to my mom and dad for all you have done to instill the confidence in me to strive for anything I set my mind to. And Steph, thanks. I know you think I got special treatment and you never got the credit you deserved, but thanks for making my bed when we were kids and taking down the trash when I forgot. You know I love you dearly.

I have to give a big shout out to Twitter. It's the reason Elizabeth and I met, and it also led me to Mack Collier and #blogchat, which gave me the notion and the tools to write a blog. That blog is what made me think I could actually write a book. Big thanks to Mack, a true southern gentleman.

Kelly Downing has been pushing me in every way for years. She's definitely not a "yes-person," and she always makes me think. Thanks for pushing me into social media, Kelly—and yes, you created a monster. Jo Newell has to get special thanks as well for assisting in many ways, but especially for her proofing of the blog and book along with P and Kelly.

Boston College also played a role in my stopping to create a curriculum that ultimately led to *Winning the Customer*. I have to first thank Will McDonough, former intern extraordinaire, Patriots employee, BC alum, and now Goldman Sachs rainmaker, who convinced Professor Maria Sannella that I would be a great lecturer in her class, which led to my teaching at BC. It was visionary of Jerry Smith, the department chair, to take a chance on a guy who never took a marketing class in his life.

I can't forget great clients and colleagues who were always there for me and allowed me to share our stories in the book. Thank you to John Holloran, Jack Shields, Michael O'Hara Lynch, John Maguire, and Joe Mariani. I also have to thank my restaurant pals Angelo Caruso and Nick Varano for allowing me to use stories of them in the book—and big thanks to Nick for hosting the *Winning the Customer* launch party at Strega Waterfront in Boston.

There were three groups of mentors and folks who took chances on me at different stages of my career, without whose support and vision I would not have been able to accomplish and experience half of what I have. In my radio and TV days, thank you to the Dean of Boston Sports Radio, Eddie Andleman, for taking me under his wing and providing an education better than any master's degree. To the Kraft family, especially Danny, Jonathan, and Mr. Kraft, you brought me into the NFL and gave me the tools, guidance, and space to soar; I will be forever grateful and will always have fond memories of working for you. Jack Blais and Joe Vrable, thank you for the encouragement and the belief in me to kick-start my entrepreneurial career. I will never forget or give up.

Before I wrap up, I have to give a big thumbs-up to my literary team. Thanks to my agent, Jeff Herman: very nice job and mission accomplished in getting me a real publisher. To vice president and group publisher of McGraw-Hill Business, Gary Krebs: thanks for believing in the concept and in me, pal. I appreciate it. It's been a wonderful experience, and you are the key component of that, but you also have a great team, and I want to specifically give a shout out to Julia Baxter and Ann Pryor in McGraw-Hill's marketing and publicity groups and to editing supervisor Pattie Amoroso, production supervisor Maureen Harper, and copyeditor Alice Manning. Ladies, you rock!

I also have to thank Heavy Advertising, especially Scott Heigelmann and Joe Del Buono, for their creativity in designing and setting up LouImbriano.com and making me look much better than I ever expected in all my photos. Thanks, gents—and Eastie Rules.

And to Elizabeth King, E~ you were unbelievable to collaborate with, and you turned my stories and experiences to gold. Thank you for all you did to make this book a reality. It would not have happened without you.

Finally, even though they are no longer with us, I have to thank my grandparents for their unwavering support and unmatched work ethic, and for showing me what my priorities should always be. I wish I could have one-tenth of their character. Miss you every day and love you much.

When I decided to leave my position as chief marketing officer for the world champion New England Patriots, I was thinking of my family. My kids were getting older, and my workday and travel schedule weren't leaving me much time to experience the kids growing up. I was out the door before 7 a.m. each day and home after 7 at night. We traveled with the team and hosted at home games. I knew that something had to give, and I decided my children were first priority.

This came at a time when I realized something else on the business end: most of the other teams in the league were missing part of the marketing and revenue-generating puzzle. It was clear that they believed that generating revenue was all about sponsorship sales, and while sponsorship is certainly a part of it, we had discovered that it's only a piece of the equation. We were successful at the Patriots because we had structured the organization so that we could build both our existing relationships and new business. We had long since abandoned the idea of just pouring more resources into new business and skimping on maintaining current business.

Knowing that other clubs and stadiums could use assistance with structuring and execution to maximize their revenues, I launched TrinityOne. Once TrinityOne was up and running, we began to notice that our methods were relevant not only to sports, but also across other industries; the principles that we had learned at the Patriots and throughout my career in sports made sense for other companies, large or small, private or public. We knew small businesses were struggling with how to put it all together, especially with limited funding and staffing.

I teach a sports marketing course at Boston College. As I created the curriculum and began to outline my thoughts and philosophies, *Winning the Customer* started to come together. Writing is a totally different animal from my normal day-to-day activities, so I knew it would be smart to have a coauthor. I talked to a few writers, but nothing seemed to click. Then I started following Elizabeth King on Twitter and noticed that she was extremely bright, funny, and a little edgy. I read her blog, StayOutofSchool.com, and liked her style. One day we were engaging in a 140-character discussion on Twitter, and I Direct Messaged her about whether she would ever consider cowriting a book. I convinced her to have a talk to chat about it. In that one phone call, I laid out my thoughts, she talked through the concept with me, and bam, just like that, we agreed to cowrite the book. Pretty cool story in itself.

Having worked in radio, in television, and for an NFL and MLS club, I had learned a particular overall approach to generating revenue: you have to *first* think of the listener, viewer, and fan, all of whom are consumers. The approach on which I've built my career stems from a unique philosophy that can work for any business. In broadcasting and team sports, we do not call our consumers "customers"; we hold them up to a higher level. It may seem like only a slight nuance, but it changes the dynamic drastically. At the radio station, *listeners* were all we could think of. We programmed every show *for* the listeners.

It's a bit different in other industries. Products are supposedly created to solve problems and provide people with solutions, but I sometimes wonder, "Did they really create that product with the consumer in mind, or did they just think it was a cool idea?" This difference in perspective also got me scratching my head about how consumer product companies provide customer service. There's a huge gap in customer relations in many industries because companies think it's all about the product rather than the customer.

In my first discussion with Andy Wasynczuk, the COO of the Patriots at the time, he told me that the Krafts thought I could create new mechanisms to bring new fans and customers to the team, but it was just as important to them that my group maintain and grow the relationships they had started building. That stuck with me for my entire time at the team. Everything we did always took both maintenance *and* growth into consideration.

Winning the Customer is all about how to maintain and grow relationships to maximize revenue. We'll talk about three key areas: (1) organizational structure and systems (The Marketing Playbook), (2) relationship building (Relationship Architecture), and (3) closing business (The Revenue Game). In order to ensure that your company maximizes revenue, all three areas must work harmoniously together.

As I love to joke, none of this is business brain surgery, but we believe that when these three areas of importance come together, you will agree that this is the best way to run your business and win the customer.

WINNING

THE

CUSTOMER

THE MARKETING PLAYBOOK

MARKETING OPERATIONS
ARE YOUR FOUNDATION

Watching an NFL game on a Sunday afternoon is one of America's ultimate pastimes. We love to grill incredible burgers, put all the kids in jerseys of their favorite players, and assemble our friends in front of the flat screen. Never mind the feeling of actually tailgating all day and witnessing the game firsthand in the stands. We love the camaraderie. We love the excitement. We love feeling that sense of identity and purpose.

But whether you're popping Doritos or on your feet yelling at the refs, it's easy to forget that you're watching a carefully choreographed marketing machine that's specifically designed to capture your imagination—and your wallet.

In fact, when it's done right, it's designed to tap into as much of your discretionary cash as possible *and* make you want to spend even more. How do I know? During my nine seasons at the Patriots, we transformed some basic marketing efforts into a revenue-generating engine, which is exactly what anyone in business and marketing should be attempting to do.

The beautiful thing about marketing a football team is that every single thing we did to generate revenue can be replicated—whether you're Johnson & Johnson or you own the Johnson Family Restaurant in a small resort town.

The challenging thing about marketing is that while it can be replicated, not very many people do so successfully.

In this section, we're going to look at an organization that's primed for generating revenue and show you how to make sure your company—whether you have a thousand employees or one—is in position to do the same. A lot of what we'll be talking about will seem obvious on the surface, but you'll probably find that what you *think* this advice means and what it *really* means can be totally different. We're going to show you those differences.

Some of what we'll tell you might seem counterintuitive, and that's fair—most people don't work this way. It may trouble you to be told that a real understanding of teamwork means not perpetually covering for people who are blowing it. It may seem unwise to treat people who are less committed to your brand better than those who are sold on it. You may find, as we did, that you have been looking for big spenders in all the wrong places.

The next three chapters will help you set up your organization to win and help you identify and understand who's already a fan of your product—and who can become one. It will also guide you toward finding those people who are absolutely dying to spend their money with you. It all starts with transferring your business from a transactional to a relationship-oriented marketing model.

Let's get started.

TRANSACTIONAL VERSUS RELATIONSHIP MARKETING MODEL

For most of the team's early existence, the New England Patriots brand was widely considered all-around flimsy: a marginal team on the playing field and a mediocre, middle-of-the-pack business organization. Everything about the organization reeked of poor business planning and knee-jerk decision making. Games were rarely sold out, and I remember as a kid following the news to see if the coming Sunday's home game was going to be blacked out on TV because of the lack of interest in attending games at Foxboro Stadium. The stadium was built on the cheap and was outdated as soon as it opened. When it rained, the concourses flooded. I'm not exaggerating when I tell you there was not one true fan amenity in that building; its most egregious flaw was posing as an NFL stadium while offering only cold aluminum benches instead of *seats*. Those metal benches epitomized price-driven decision making and made it blatantly clear that no thought had been given to the fans.

Today, just about anyone who is familiar with the team, fan or not, views the organization as a model franchise—both on the field and in its business structure and execution—and it has the *Forbes* magazine cover story to prove it. As with the vast majority of successful businesses, transforming it from so-so to a powerhouse did not occur overnight; it took years of careful reorganization from the ground up (and the top down) to reinvent both the brand and the business model to the level of excellence it now enjoys.

When I joined the New England Patriots back in 1997, the transformation had already been set in motion. The rebuilding of the organization had begun, initiated shortly after the Kraft family purchased the team and grounded in the family's clear vision of the team's future. Because the Krafts had owned Foxboro Stadium prior to buying the team, they enjoyed an inside position; they were primed to apply their business success in other industries to the team, and they had a real understanding of how to turn the franchise around. When the Kraft family bought the team, it focused on cleaning up the image and experience of going to games at Foxboro Stadium. That transition was going to require migrating the team's business practices from a transactional to a relationship-oriented model.

Whether you realize it or not, you're already deeply familiar with transactional business models. Those folks selling bouquets of flowers on the street at stoplights are the simplest example. As you slow down to stop at the red light, they come to your window, hoping you will buy a bunch for $10. If you do, they grab the ten-spot, hand you your flowers, and you're off. They are, too—in hopes of landing their next sucker. This is a purely transactional sale. It's not quite so cut-and-dried in the context of an enormous organization like the Patriots, but the model is transactional just the same. Let's look at one specific area of the organization so you can get a better idea of what I mean: sponsorship.

The reason companies sponsor the team is to use the Patriots' identity and assets for their own branding and marketing initiatives. Before the rebuilding of the organization, selling a sponsorship package would go something like this: the sponsorship sales reps would get a meeting with a company they felt would buy in, show up at the meeting, and plunk down a package of team and stadium assets like signs, media, and logo rights. The sales team's approach was to always focus on selling the inventory that it had in stock, so if it hadn't sold enough, say, signs for the year, that would be the first thing on the table for sale to a potential sponsor—whether or not it was relevant to that company. The ways in which the company could use the inventory were not an important part of the equation. The team just wanted to sell its inventory and was focused on getting the sale.

Once the transaction was complete, the sales reps were off to the next sale. It was almost like, "Thanks for signing the contract. See you in three years!" (at the deal's expiration date). The process was all about closing business and not about producing results for the customers, which, at the time, was a typical way of doing business in the NFL and other leagues. Unfortunately, some teams *still* operate this way, not recognizing that transactional business is built around short-term gain and sacrifices long-term vision and sustainability.

The biggest issue with this approach was that when the contract expired, evaluating whether the inventory had helped the sponsor see a return on its investment was about as reliable as flipping a coin. Let's face it: it is pretty difficult to determine whether a sign in a stadium actually drove business to your company. Come budget evaluation time, things that aren't easily quantified are easier to do without. If the added value couldn't be proven, sponsors might not renew, which further forced the staff to operate in a reactionary, year-to-year selling method. They continuously worked to replace lost sponsors, each rep a hamster running on its wheel—there was plenty of motion, but no progress.

A cycle like this obviously hampers revenue growth; it's a struggle just to keep up with the status quo. At a football team, revenue-generation plans like this are disastrous for the team because the marketing group ends up being dependent on wins to fuel the team's financial advances—when the team wins, it makes money selling more merchandise, tickets, and sponsorship. The problem is that a sports team's winning is unpredictable, and the folks in marketing have zero control over the performance of the team. Having a marketing plan based on wins and losses will cause you to lose revenue. It's a stupid plan.

Dependence on the team's win record is not a great strategy for generating recurring revenue, and the same is true for any other business. You sell a product or service, but no organization should rely purely on the validity of the product to generate revenue. No matter how significant the brand, it's the relationship that the organization forms with its consumers to cause continued revenue growth that drives revenue. We're going to get into how to generate revenue beyond your product in great detail in this book, but implementing a business structure that supports relational business is the first step in getting there.

DESIGNING A BUSINESS OPERATIONS MODEL BUILT FOR REVENUE

A product alone does not create fans of a brand; it's the harmonious dance between the product and its positioning that does so. The teamwork between product design and marketing is crucial to ensure maximum growth. While the owners of the Patriots were working to rebuild the product, the team, and the stadium, our group was charged with developing a marketing structure that would win customers, regardless of the team's wins and losses.

I want to pause here because I realize that it's easy to believe that winning on the field solves everything. Yes, winning on the field is awesome, but without the right structure and plan in place, it's impossible to capitalize on those wins. Similarly, you may have the best product for sale, a product that's far better than your closest competitor's, but if your business structure isn't built to support it efficiently, you are not marketing it properly, and you're neglecting to create relationships with your consumer, you will never maximize your revenue opportunity. Always remember, revenue *begins* with the product; it doesn't end there.

It was clear from the outset at the Patriots that we had to build a different model to secure financial sustainability—we had to become relationship-oriented. Hoping that we'd have enough sponsors at every contract expiration just wasn't going to work. With the new, relational approach, we still marketed team assets like signs, media, and logo rights, but we sold them just to recognize revenue. The real business deal was to identify the sponsors' needs and goals and show how we could help accomplish them. Our job became not to "sell" anything; our primary function became *to help our partners do business.*

To do this effectively, we first had to change the structure of our department and how we operated to get into position to build strong relationships; everyone's job description and list of responsibilities changed so that we could invest our efforts in learning about our partners' businesses and what would help them succeed, which included learning as much as possible about the individuals within the company. We stopped being transactional salespeople and evolved into relationship architects.

Changing How We Thought about Teamwork

Again, the first step was changing our structure, job functions, and protocols, so that's where we're beginning in the book. In the mid-1990s, the marketing department of the New England Patriots had around six staff members, and everyone did a little bit of everything, helping one another out. That sounds noble, but it was actually incredibly inefficient. Salespeople would prospect for new business, help coordinate contract execution, and hand out giveaways at the stadium gates. Everyone doing everything prevents an organization from reaching its full potential. If you are a member of the team and you are doing everything, how can you possibly perform your main function properly and consistently? The belief is that the person who has the "teamwork" gene is always there to help others and make sure the team is successful, regardless of who is doing the work and how it gets done. Folks, it's time to wake up and smell the Dunkin' Donuts coffee: that's not teamwork, that's disorganization.

Even the cavemen understood this principle: everyone had his own specific skill set and excelled in a specific area. Not to oversimplify, but in caveman days, there were hunters, gatherers/preparers, and cooks. The hunters were the strongest, fastest members of the community, and they would battle every day to bring home enough food to feed everyone in their clan. Hunters would hand off their spoils to the next group, who, while the hunters were out doing their job, gathered all the necessary ingredients, skinned and prepared the fresh meat, and handed it off to those who cooked it and served it to the clan. Everyone had a specific job that allowed the others to accomplish their jobs to the very best of their ability. Imagine if the hunter had had to do everything; the community would probably have starved. Survival was predicated on everyone doing *only* his own job.

A similarly structured marketing group allows an organization to flourish. The marketing team we were building was focused on everyone doing her own job to the best of her ability and pulling together for a common goal. It was *not* about encouraging the practice of being the superstar who fills in all the gaps and covers up the deficiencies of an organization. It was designed specifically to allow the salespeople, the "hunters," to maximize how much revenue and how many new deals they could bring into the organization. Then, we assembled a marketing ops team to specifically support them.

If a keeper ran all over the pitch trying to make every play, who would protect the net? Can a quarterback throw a pass and then catch it as well? Of course not. Coach Bill Parcells used to make a statement that has stuck with me for many years: "Know your role." I've heard the stories so many times about Coach Parcells approaching a defensive lineman and saying, "Your job this Sunday is to put number 76 on his ass. Forget about the ball. Forget about the quarterback. You will be successful if, on every play, I look over and see number 76 on his ass."

The coach instructed each player in a similar fashion, providing him with his own mission that strategically fit piece by piece with the overall game plan. He knew that if everyone played his role and executed as instructed, the team would win. I never witnessed the pep talk first-hand, but the concept has stuck with me and makes total, logical sense.

The New England Patriots have won three Super Bowls, but that first win was the one that caught people outside the organization off guard. However, I'm positive that Bill Belichick, our coach during those victories, was the least surprised because he knew that the players understood their individual roles and that their collaboration resulted in a powerful team. I remember him being so calm and confident the week prior to that first Super Bowl victory in New Orleans over the St. Louis Rams. Watching him stay so relaxed, I kept thinking, "We are going to win this one. The coach knows we are going to win this game." Of course, he didn't *actually* know, but a feeling permeated our headquarters at the Fairmount Hotel that he had confidence that his team would perform with the characteristics that embodied teamwork. The St. Louis Rams were the favorites going into the game; heck, their offense was called "the Greatest Show on Turf." We supposedly had "no right" to be in the game; we were "lucky" and had "no chance" of winning. Through all the hype and disbelief, Coach was right. He'd organized the team to win.

So teamwork, first and foremost, means knowing your role and executing it to your fullest ability. That was the first philosophy that we brought to the marketing department: you display teamwork when you get your job done the way it was laid out in the planning process. Then, and only then, should you attempt to take on any other duties or assist in any other capacity. In the case of the lineman whose job was to put number 76 on his ass—sure, once number 76 was eighty-sixed, he should pummel the quarterback into the ground if he's there for the taking. But never, and I must repeat never, avoid your primary responsibility and the reason that you are a part of the team. If your teammate is slacking, you are not helping by doing his job for him and hiding a weakness on the team.

Don't Cover Up the Weak Spots

In order to coach, lead, or teach effectively, it is imperative to expose the weaknesses in an organization. Covering up deficiencies only disguises areas that need to be improved and fixed. Filling those gaps is *not* good teamwork if doing so leaves gaps and long-term problems unsolved.

In fact, the consummate team player does not always pick up the slack. I remember always being frustrated when I was in radio because I worked so hard and other folks breezed through, riding on the work that I and others did. At times they were applauded and given opportunities and greater responsibilities simply because they had a knack for catching the eye of the boss. One very smart mentor and friend, John Maguire, GM of Sports Radio WEEI at the time, once told me, "Don't let that make you crazy; sometimes you just have to let things unravel." I always wanted to be "Mr. Fix-It" because I truly wanted the group to succeed, but assuming that role was only a short-term solution and was not the behavior of a true team player—or a sign of a well-designed team.

Teamwork takes discipline and knowing your role and the roles of the others on the team. Just because you know the other roles, you shouldn't necessarily fill them. If you do help out, make sure you've tended to your own responsibilities first and be sure the deficient group member knows that he needs to step it up, even though you did have his back. Teamwork leads to victories and successes, if you know what it truly takes to be a team.

MANAGEMENT: REINFORCING AND DEFINING ROLES

At this point, it should be clear that while we were changing the structure of the Patriots' business and marketing organization, we were perpetually reinforcing everyone's new roles and how those roles fit into the overall plan. We also recognized that six people in the department were just too few to accomplish all that we were charged with accomplishing.

This is crucial for successful marketing: you could have all the best, coolest ideas to position your brand, but if you cannot bring the concepts to life as they are drawn up in your playbook, then the ideas are for naught. My grandfather used to always say to me, "It's not a great idea unless it actually accomplishes something." He was so right. I have borrowed that thought and applied it to our approach to business. I always say: "If an idea doesn't generate revenue or build relationships, it's a bad idea."

Defining Your Structure

In order to get the most out of your employees or your "team," you have to put each member in a position where she can win. To do this, there needs to be a clear, top-down understanding of the structure of the organization, the protocols, and each individual role within the structure. A lot of people balk at the mention of this kind of rigidity; organizational layers can seem like they'll bog things down with process and red tape. However, great organization and structure expedite.

There's a scene in *Days of Thunder* that I love and use often when I'm trying to stress the importance of doing things within the plan and everyone understanding the importance of her role. Robert Duval's character, the crew chief for a NASCAR team, is explaining to Tom Cruise, the driver, that driving as fast as he possibly can will not win races. I know this doesn't sound logical at first, but as Duval's character explains, racing is more about how everything all works together. The team loses if there is a breakdown, if one area is not in sync with all the others. Duval explains to Cruise that if he drove 50 laps Duval's way (slower) and 50 laps Cruise's way (pedal to the metal), Duval's method would win every time. They go through the exercise in the movie, and at the end of the two sets of 50 laps, Cruise yields a faster time driving more slowly, just as Duval assured him. The reason, Duval explains, is that driving as fast as possible causes the temperature of the tires to rise; they begin to melt and subsequently become slick. Just like when you're driving on ice in the wintertime, the tires spin faster, but the vehicle doesn't travel as fast. It's the same in business: if everyone is off doing his own thing as fast as he can, there may be lots of motion, but is there true progress?

When I first took over marketing for the New England Revolution, the business plan was basically "run all over the place"; so much of the group's efforts were reactionary. It *seemed* as if people were hustling about, but they were exactly like those spinning, melting tires. Their plan was to throw as much mud as possible up against the wall and see what stuck. The energy was great, but the progress was weak. Sure, when you're a start-up, you do need a little bit of that "just roll up your sleeves and do it" attitude, but as with most things, a balanced effort will get you much further. We had to shift the model so that the energy was still there, but planned and targeted more directly.

Don't get me wrong: I'm not a big believer in overanalyzing. I once told a former boss that by the time he finished analyzing how to proceed, I'd already be 90 percent complete. I believe in instituting business processes and structures that perform reliably on their own and implementing strategy that allows everyone to maximize her efforts and make great decisions in her own position on the team. Being decisive now with 85 percent certainty is much more beneficial to growth than being 100 percent sure nine months from now, if you have a properly structured and trained group.

Putting People in Position to Win

We put a plan and a process in place that allowed us to have further range and accuracy. The first steps we took were stressing that salespeople's primary function was to go out and procure new business. No longer were they to take up valuable revenue-generating time handing out items on game day or working with clients to figure out the appropriate shade of PMS colors for their signage. We now had another group that became responsible for that process; it was this group's job to guarantee the proper execution of the sponsorship element of a deal. In fact, we subdivided the marketing department at both the Patriots and the Revolution into two groups: New Business (Sales) and Marketing Operations. Just like the cavemen: hunters and preparers/cooks. We paired this restructuring with a new, automated marketing database system to propel our group to growth.

The automated system set the table for flawless execution and interaction with our clients and customers. We painstakingly worked with

IT, Accounting, and Legal for six months to create an automated system that allowed us to build better relationships with our clients and execute flawlessly and to the fullest. When we were finished, this system and structure allowed us to expand our efforts and generate more revenue.

Initially, we built the system around delivering sponsorship packages to new clients. The new process went as follows: a salesperson began building relationships with potential clients. Once the timing was appropriate, he built a sponsorship package by selecting the elements in the ONYX system that we had created. Once the package was complete and in the system, Gail, who was our database/inventory manager, received a notice. She made sure that the items in the package were available and that all the details and pricing were correct. If they were available, she approved the package, and a notice went to a sales assistant to build a presentation.

The normal sales process with the client commenced once there was agreement on the package between the team and the potential sponsor, the sales executive advanced it in the process, and it landed on my desk for review. Once it was approved, at a click of a button, the appropriate fulfillment, accounting, and legal people all received clearance and began working on their particular areas to help finalize the deal and be in a position to fully execute it once it was signed. I'm not going to go through every detail, but I believe it's easy to see that a simple, organized system was in place, and the structure and protocols that were followed ensured flawless execution.

"Have a system in place" is not earth-shattering advice. Either companies do the "everyone does everything" thing or they have a system. But let's be real: for every company that's getting it right, there are many that are getting it wrong. A lot of companies believe in their salespeople and leave it at that; in fact, most people think revenue generation is all about selling. I'm here to tell you that that is inaccurate.

Business development is not just about building a great sales team, just like having a great quarterback alone does not win you Super Bowls. To prove this, I only have to mention one name to NFL fans: Dan Marino. For those who are unfamiliar with that name, Dan Marino is a Hall of Fame quarterback and perhaps one of the best passers of all time. Does he have a Super Bowl ring? No. The biggest injustice in the NFL is that I have three Super Bowl rings and Dan Marino has none. It takes a team to win, not one superstar. You may have the best sales talent around, but without the proper marketing machine behind them, you are not maximizing your potential revenue.

Key System Elements

Here are the key things you want to look for to ensure that your system is set up so that you can be sure it works, and works well.

1. A Balance of Management Depth If you have a fairly large organization with one boss to whom everyone answers, you already have a solid indicator that things are probably not as efficient as they could be. That being said, many organizations are actually *more* structured than is really necessary, with multiple levels of management that duplicate each other. Leaders need to think about strategy and vision, and the people underneath them need to think about execution. Everyone else also works toward that execution. You want to create a structure that has only enough levels to keep employees focused on their goals and is not so subdivided that no one understands the big picture. The key is to understand that you cannot have multiple silos in which everyone works solely on her own agenda; that kind of disconnect guarantees that the plans and goals are never completely fulfilled and executed.

2. An Appropriately Subdivided Organization I always like to see one head, multiple departments, and multiple subdivisions under them *sliced in accordance with job function.* I know this may seem routine, like Business 101, but I can't tell you the number of organizations we consult with that are structural catastrophes. Because we sign confidentiality agreements, I obviously can't tell you names, but I'm sure you have seen it: Bob has been with the company for 20 years, and over that time he's assumed more responsibility. His department has continually taken on new functions, and we're left asking ourselves why Bob in Legal handles picking out the rugs and furniture for the new offices. I know it sounds far-fetched, but believe me, this is a real example. This seems harmless, but when Bob is picking out furniture, who is writing up that new deal that just came in?

3. New Functions Assigned to the Right People—Even If That Means Hiring When I was at the Patriots, Bank of Boston, a fairly large and well-run organization, was one of our sponsors. Its community relations department was running its sports sponsorships. While I never directly asked why, I assume that when the bank did its first sponsorship, someone said, "Give it to Community Relations. It does some charitable sponsorship. Sports sponsorships must be similar." Again, I don't know that this is exactly what happened, but it is clearly unwise to delegate this function in that manner. When something new comes into play, it's not always best to just give it to a group you trust or an area you think can "handle" it. The skill set of someone in Community Relations, although perhaps similar to that of the people in Sponsorship, is not the *same* as that of someone whose expertise is in sponsorship management.

The skill set of a killer salesperson/closer is quite different from the skill set of a disciplined operations person. It's a common mistake to confuse responsibility like this in sports marketing in particular—people think that because they like sports, they understand how to market using sports teams and venues. Just because you like something doesn't mean you're good at it. Keep in mind that salespeople are addicted to the close and will quite often offer and promise things that are unobtainable in order to close a deal. Marketing operations folks wouldn't stray that way, but they most likely lack the necessary skills to be a closer.

As management, make sure that you're always considering real skill sets before you assign new business elements. Everyone needs to be in a place where he's strongest, and then your structure balances and checks the behaviors within your department.

EXTRA POINTS
For some sample organization charts for large and small businesses, tap into http://louimbriano.com/ winningthecustomer-reference. There you'll find great tools to help you structure your own organization.

Once you've designed your own system and it's in place, it's important that you lay out expectations to your team. It's very easy for employees to not "get" what you are trying to accomplish, and most of the time this is because it has never been clearly laid out for them. Whether you are an employer or an employee, you need to understand this next set of principles.

Again, the big problem is that employees have a tendency to focus on the wrong things. When someone gets a new job in any industry or organization, there is so much "new" to absorb that it can be overwhelming, and it's easy to end up lacking a sense of pointed direction, even if the company has a training program. It's also easy for upper management to lose sight of reality: just because managers clearly understand what they are trying to accomplish, they believe those ideas permeate throughout the organization with the same clarity. Usually, they *don't*.

The larger the organization, the greater the distance between its philosophy and its execution.

How to Thrive in a Structure as an Employee

As I began to develop the structure of my staff at the New England Patriots, I began simultaneously writing down thoughts about the organization that, as a nonmanagement employee, I would want to know and advice that would be helpful to members of the staff as we went forward. I mapped out four tips for employees to empower them to navigate the work, understand the goals of the company, and create a solid relationship with their employer. Following are four guidelines that should lead all employees, no matter what company they work for, to success.

1. Understand the Expectations of the People You Work For Your job description is a starting point, but it never fully captures what is expected of you. Ask questions of your direct supervisor to get a clearer picture of those tasks that are expected of you. Start by ensuring that you always know your individual short- and long-term goals.

2. Know the Philosophies and the Goals of the Organization You Work For Many employees stop at their own goals for career development and their job descriptions, thinking that that's all that is necessary for success. *Wrong!* You have to understand what the company is trying to accomplish and the manner in which it wants to operate. In many companies, the details necessary to fully capture this information will have to be sought out; they're the kinds of things being discussed in the management meetings. Unfortunately, the real goals are rarely handed to you in one neat little package, even in company training programs.

Ask questions of your supervisor and other leaders within the organization to get a clear picture of its goals and, just as important, its overall philosophy on how to operate. Quite often, there is a disconnection between what the upper management/leadership wants and how employees view what it wants. Make it your job to seek out the goals of the company and get in line with them.

3. Overdeliver on Expectations in Accordance with the Philosophy Understanding your goals and the organization's philosophy puts you in a better position to be a great employee, but to achieve, you must make it your goal to *exceed* expectations. This is how you get noticed and become someone who is seen as reliable and needed. If you master this, you will move up in the ranks of any company, usually very quickly. Always set loftier goals for yourself than the organization expects of you. Hold yourself to a higher standard. This puts the control of your success in your own hands.

4. Never Assume Entitlement There are a bunch of so-called superstars out there who believe that they can do no wrong. Once they start accomplishing and climbing the ladder, they start approaching their work with an elitist attitude. A surefire way to destroy all the equity you have built in an organization is to assume that because you have been an asset, you are now entitled to privileges. You may have earned the respect and gratitude of the company, but you are entitled to nothing. Hopefully, you will be justly rewarded for your services. But if you feel you are not, take your skills and proper attitude to another organization that will. In any event, never adopt the attitude that you "deserve" anything, because that attitude erases all the good you have done up to that point. If you truly are all that you think you are, you will get what you deserve.

No matter what organization or person you work for, if you approach your job and career with these four guidelines in mind and consistently deliver on them, you will be successful. Most people just fly by the seats of their pants when they go to work every day. No plan, no reason, just the same routine: up in the morning, breakfast, traffic, and plop down at your desk. Don't fall into that trap. You, and only you, are in control of your ultimate success.

Put the CMO in Charge of Both Sales and Marketing

This all leads to my preferred philosophy on the structure of any marketing group within a corporation. I am not a huge fan of having separate marketing and sales departments: Sales is a function of Marketing, not a separate arm of the business. When I worked in radio and TV I was always frustrated by the corporate structure that kept these departments separate; I've always believed that one group would be more synergistic and effective. Since then, I consistently migrate toward establishing one leader who understands the importance and balance of Sales and Marketing working together.

Transactional business models scream to me that the departments are separate. When I was in radio, we were always saying, "This is sports radio, we're men—Jiffy Lube should be doing business with us!" It's a totally transactional approach based on assumptions. But, when we actually *went* to Jiffy Lube, we were told that the company's target audience is women and that its brand is all about making people's lives easier.

As you remember from the beginning of the chapter, maximizing sales is reliant on migrating to a relationship-oriented model, in which case Sales and Marketing must be unified. If the CMO understands how Sales and Marketing dance together, you will see significant changes and growth not only in revenue but also in customer satisfaction. In the relationship model, selling is not the theme; building is the primary focus.

Later in the book, we'll explore further how this structural, systematic change in our approach laid the groundwork that allowed us to retain sponsors after contract expiration, grow relationships organically, and gain additional partnerships regardless of our wins and losses on the field and in spite of the dilapidated stadium we started in. You'll see how this change in our operational approach allowed the organization to grow sponsorship revenue more than 85 percent. The strategic changes that increased revenue had nothing to do with the team, were not about wins, and had nothing to do with building a state-of-the-art stadium. Again, our marketing approach and structure *alone* allowed us to flourish and experience growth in both revenue and the number of partners we had.

More important, we were positioned for enormous growth when the team did start winning consistently and when we built Gillette Stadium. In fact, after we built the new stadium and won Super Bowls, marketing revenue increased *more than 600 percent*. The structure put us in a position to win and capitalize on the team's success, ultimately realizing the ownership's original vision. It's important to be clear on how unusual this is: there are many other teams that do not increase revenues by even 25 percent after winning championships on the field. The Super Bowl didn't create the 600 percent increase; the structure that was in place prior to the victories allowed it to become possible. The combination of proper structure, planning, and an incredible product is lightning in a bottle and the true way to maximize growth.

Think Like a Structured CMO Even If You're a Team of One

So far we've talked a lot about reorganizing large teams of people and creating direction and focus for each of the employees on the team. When you're a small company and you have to take on multiple roles for cost cutting and survival, that doesn't mean you need to multitask yourself into inefficiency. I went from running a 40-person department to running a 4-person consultancy with TrinityOne. Because we're a small shop, I serve not only as the CEO but also as creative director and new business executive. I also empty the trash.

Wearing a number of hats is common in a small business, but just because you are responsible for multiple tasks doesn't mean the situation has to overwhelm you. I got caught in that trap in the beginning: I would be working on one project, and then a 10 a.m. meeting would arrive and I would stop to have the meeting. Once the meeting ended, I'd restart the project I'd been working on, but invariably I'd get interrupted by one of the employees—it was stop and go all day long. Inevitably I'd never fully accomplish all I had set out to, and I would have to stay late or reprioritize for the next day.

Then it hit me. I'm in charge of my workweek, and it should be planned out more precisely. Just as big companies have departments, I decided to departmentalize my workweek. I told my assistant that I was no longer available for meetings on Mondays and Fridays. Those days were reserved for writing, thinking, and planning. Tuesdays and Thursdays were slated for "outside meetings and calls," and I was available to meet from 6 a.m. to 10 p.m. That may sound like an incredibly long day, but I wanted all outside meetings to be only on those two days. Lately Tuesday has been transformed into new business day. And finally, Wednesday became my day for internal meetings and discussions with my staff. We always keep the weekends to pick up slack if necessary, which is possible because we've designed our business so that we can do our jobs anywhere.

This exact structure may not work for your company and what you do, but departmentalizing the week will definitely allow you to be more productive. Look at the functions you need to perform and slot them into the days where they fit best. Regardless of the business you are in, this type of structure will help you maximize your ability to achieve your goals and generate more revenue.

CREATING CONNECTION ACROSS DEPARTMENTS: CUSTODIANS OF THE BRAND

The relationship-oriented model cannot be left to your marketing and sales department alone; the theme must saturate the entire organization, and all employees must become custodians of the brand. Every brand must have a brand positioning statement. While every company's statement will be different, the point of the brand positioning statement is to outline and articulate what separates your company from all the other companies in your market. This statement is what you'll use to drive the vision of every employee in your company.

Most organizations are departmentalized for strength and efficiency, but the big weakness that creeps in is that each department begins focusing only on its own objectives. Now, accomplishing your assigned goals is imperative, but the rest of the organization mustn't be negatively affected if you do. If you're not careful, that's entirely possible. All members of an organization need to be cognizant not only of their own department's goals, but also of the goals of all other departments and the organization as a whole.

In a larger organization, it can be tough to make sure that every department is mindful of the others, but a great place to start is with the idea that every employee should view him- or herself as a custodian of the brand. Let's look at one very small, often overlooked piece that can absolutely kill the efforts of the other departments: Reception.

When I was in radio, I used to call the Red Sox all the time to book players and executives to appear on the show I produced. The elderly woman answering the main line used to pick up the phone and screech, "*RED SOX*." Believe me, seeing it in print just doesn't do it justice. I would then ask for the person I wanted to speak with, and I would be immediately put on hold (almost before I finished). Whoa! The first person you reached when you called the Sox organization, the gatekeeper, was obviously not trained in customer service or relationship building.

When I took over marketing for the New England Patriots, I began lobbying for my department to run Reception, which I viewed as the window to the organization. The person stationed at the reception desk creates the first impression of the inside of the organization, whether someone calls or shows up for a visit. Marketers get so caught up in the external perception of their brand that they often lose sight of the potential impact that a glimpse of the inner workings of an organization can have on outsiders. The Pats' reception wasn't nearly as bad as it was at the Red Sox, but I saw it as an opportunity to separate us from the rest of the pack. Initially, there was huge resistance because it was traditionally a stadium operational function and, as in most companies, things can get territorial. I was of the mindset that *everyone* worked for Marketing (and mentioned it quite often, making me less than popular with other department heads) because virtually all levels of the organization interacted with fans, our *consumers*.

The best-case scenario would have been to convince Operations to adopt the concept that everyone needed to be a custodian of the brand in an afternoon meeting, but that change was going to take a bit longer.

Acquiring Reception was a more realistic approach: it could get the ball rolling and could help us prove the overall value of the philosophy. I was on a mission to have Reception fall under Marketing. After a few years of my relentlessly and opportunistically pushing the idea, Jonathan Kraft, a brilliant businessman who could run any company, agreed and told me that Reception was ours and would now hit our budget. The budget change was a great motivator for Operations to relinquish control.

I had a concept in mind, so paying for Reception was not a deterrent. The problem with a job that primarily consists of answering phones and connecting callers to others is that the employee often falls into the trap of boredom—or worse, thinking that his job is meaningless. To combat this perception, we broke the mold for our hiring model.

We didn't hire full-time staff for the role. Now that Reception was a marketing function, we integrated it into our internship program. We found a bright, motivated group of college interns and charged them with being reception staff for a few hours a week; they'd work the rest of their hours on other marketing functions. We trained them to embrace the job as a marketer and to "own" the position. It was made clear that how they handled their function at Reception and as the gatekeeper of the organization would be a key factor in potentially getting an offer to become a full-time employee.

As a result, we always had a motivated, friendly, knowledgeable receptionist on duty who embraced the position with a positive and helpful attitude. These new gatekeepers were charged with learning as much about the organization as possible. They became true custodians of the brand. Once everything was in the place, the first voice you heard as you entered the Patriots organization was welcoming and inviting—the absolute opposite of what you encountered when you called the "RED SOX" in the 1990s.

Going Beyond Reception

Many companies operate as though only those people who interface with customers need to be trained in customer service or be encouraged to be custodians of the brand. It's a dangerous management decision to make. Backroom folks who never engage with consumers are most likely affecting *something* that customers will come in contact with. To fully win the customer over and over, everyone needs to adopt this ideology and consider how her actions affect the customer's experience. Whether you're the janitor or the CEO, you must be a custodian of the brand.

Every person in every job position has to understand that it is not just about whether he executes his function; it's also about *how* it is performed. Anyone who has been to Disney World understands this concept. It's extremely unusual to see a piece of trash on the ground at Disney because Disney is the master of instilling the importance of how things are done the Disney way. Quite literally, the custodians at Disney are incredible custodians of the Disney brand. Structure and protocols that ensure adherence to the brand philosophy are key—they are the foundation for all of your marketing and sales efforts.

When everybody within your organization thinks like a custodian of the brand, you'll find it easy to begin to take the next step: turning *customers* into *fans* of your brand. Let's face facts here; all these efforts have one endgame in mind, generating more revenue for your company. Don't be ashamed or embarrassed to state this inside the company. *You are in business to make money.* Once your internal structure is set up to support maximized revenue generation, it's time to start looking at your fans: who they are, how they want you to treat them, and how to create even more of them.

CONSUMER AFFINITY: MAKING FANS OF YOUR CUSTOMERS

Having built my entire career in sports, I have come to appreciate that the consumers for the organizations I have worked for have been fans. The real power of having *fans* instead of merely *customers* didn't truly dawn on me until I had been through a couple of seasons with the Patriots. It really began to sink in as we created new events: not only were fans enthralled with the thought of the team and everything associated with it, but their appetite to consume anything and everything Patriots was insatiable. That's when it really hit me: *fans* are *consumers.* Sure, I always knew they spent money to see the team, but it's deeper than that. Fans become *consumed* with the team. Once that clicked, I never looked at fans the same way again.

Thinking about promotions that we could create that would compel fans to spend more money with the team became a sport in itself. Like clockwork, the more we gave them what they wanted, the more they bought. Turning fans into consumers was not exactly a grueling task— after all, they were already sold on the team. When I left the team, the concept of turning consumers at any company into fans really intrigued me. Talk about purchase power if we could accomplish just that.

CREATING FANS

Guess what: sports teams and rock bands have not cornered the market on fandom. Nike, Porsche, and Coca-Cola are just a few of the bigger brands that have made fans out of their consumers. Your company, no matter how large or small it may be, or whether it sells business-to-consumer or business-to-business, must put a strategy into place to transform your customers into fans. The passion that comes from a new fan is powerful and always leads to significant revenue growth.

Be forewarned, though: if you're going to create new fans, you have to accept the increased responsibility that comes with them, because your brand becomes personal to a fan and you will be held to a higher standard. Look at the backlash that Coke experienced when it introduced New Coke to its consumers. Coke was not true to its brand or to the relationship it had built with its fans. This disenchantment eroded the relationship, and therefore the business, significantly. It took Coca-Cola a while to rebuild those relationships and recover lost revenues. There are probably still some former Coke consumers that never returned because of this breach of trust.

Even with the added responsibility and potential pitfalls, every company's goal should be to convert its consumers into fans. Just as in sports, you never know when your competitor is going to make improvements to beat you. Creating fans is a great way to protect against that threat: the relationship you form with your consumers will help you minimize the downside during the lean times and maximize the upside when times are good. You have to consistently evolve your brand so your consumers are fans of the brand; you want them always wanting to see what's next.

Apple's team has mastered continuously evolving to be exactly what Apple's consumers want it to be. Apple is not a sports franchise, but it understands that if you make your consumers fans, their passion for the product will keep them on the edge of their seats waiting for the next big play. Apple is always improving its products and knows exactly how to market its brand and its new gadgets. How does it know? Apple listens to and forges relationships with its customers. The iPad marketing campaign was so outstanding that there were lines of people who wanted to be the first to get an iPad waiting for stores to open. And then again, after tweaks and adjustments based on consumers' needs, the iPad 2 was released, and flocks of consumers *again* waited in line to get the new product. Don't be fooled: these are not just consumers. These are fans of Apple and its products.

What happens at Apple stores is the same phenomenon as when your home team wins the pennant and fans camp out all night in line in order to get tickets for the playoffs. Their passion for their team causes them to behave as though nothing matters but being there to see their team achieve a championship. If you want to continuously win the customer, you have to turn your customers into fans and build that kind of intense relationship with them.

In order to harness that power of converting fans' passion into revenue, you have to recognize which consumers are actually fans. Since you're probably not a rock band, your consumers will not be walking into your establishment wearing a concert T-shirt, screaming your company's name, and throwing their undergarments at you (although it would be comical if Frank at the cash register had some boxers thrown at him: "*Yeah*, Staples, I love your ink!"). For the rest of us, pinpointing fans is a bit more work, but it's incredibly worthwhile.

Identifying Fans of Your Company

Identifying fans of your company is important to growing revenues, and yet many companies, even big ones, squander opportunities to do so. There are always signals and signs that indicate that people are fans of your company. Some obvious signs in this day and age include people "liking" your fan page on Facebook or following you on Twitter. There are reasons why people take those actions: they are indicating they have a stronger interest in your brand. This small action is opening the door for further interaction with your company.

However, consumers often make much bigger commitments and send louder signals indicating that they are fans. With team sports, it's a bit easier to see: if an individual buys a jersey in the team's pro shop, there's a pretty good chance that this person or someone close to him is a fan of the team at some level. The mere purchase doesn't indicate his level of fandom, but you know that he is in orbit around your brand. There are indicators for every company and every brand out there; you just have to know what to look for and what to do with the information. Take Starbucks or Dunkin' Donuts, for example. People are in and out of those shops on a daily basis. There are as many coffee cups on the train as there are people, and most of them bear the Dunkin' or Starbucks logo. Some people just have the paper cups with the sleeves so they don't burn their fingers, but others may have a nicer, reusable version that they use every morning. In sports, we call those "souvenir cups."

If people are making the commitment to buy a Dunkin' Donuts travel cup, it's definitely an indicator of fandom on some level. The questions are: at exactly what level are these people and what do you as a marketer do with that information? Not to act on this knowledge is a mistake companies make every day—even successful ones like Dunkin' Donuts and Starbucks.

There are indicators that there are fans all around your brand, and quite often there is no follow-up. The key to a fan indication is to capture the moment and a little data along with it. As I said before, it's easier to spot a fan if you are the Patriots (a guy painting his face blue and wearing a number 12 jersey is a pretty clear sign), but even teams have to capture data. At the Patriots Pro Shop, we collected information when folks made a purchase, which is becoming quite common in many retail outlets. I just bought a watch for my wife at Tourneau, and the first question I was asked was whether I'd shopped there before. The salesperson took down my info, and just like that, I am in the store's database.

This is a great start, but what the company does with the info is a whole other story. At the Patriots, not only were we collecting info, but we also worked with Adidas and Reebok to put little tags on the jerseys with other Patriots-related offers. For example, we did one cross promotion where an extra tag on the jersey pointed buyers to an offer for *Patriots Football Weekly*, our team newspaper. The tag was right there, plain as day. It's just another way to dig deeper into people's fandom and increase revenues.

Indicators like these are just as important for the coffee purveyors. The key for them is collecting data. Given that someone's buying a "souvenir cup" is a good indicator that she is a fan of the brand at some level, the company should never be satisfied simply with the thought that she might come back. It's crucial to continually build on this potential fandom. The strength you can see at Dunkin' and Starbucks is that they have a product at a price point that's cost-effective *and* very conducive to enticing folks to give up information. When someone purchases a souvenir cup at Starbucks, she should immediately be offered her next cup of coffee for free in exchange for providing her name and e-mail address. Once the information is collected, the customer will be e-mailed a voucher for a free cup of coffee. The person who bought that cup will in all probability want that free cup of coffee enough to give a legitimate e-mail address. That simple, cost-effective offer will lead Starbucks to a better understanding of that particular consumer's enthusiasm for its product. Starbucks can track whether that fan redeems the coupon for free coffee and further engage with that fan to understand how big a fan and how *loyal* a customer she is and, more important, can become.

As a company, your goal is to identify your customers' level of commitment to your brand. To do so, you first have to identify the indicators that a consumer is a fan, and second, you have to know what steps to take to understand at what level of fandom he resides. Unless you're shilling coffee, you're probably not selling cups with logos on them, so you need to keep your eyes open for indicators that may not be as blatant as a souvenir cup purchase but that give you the same sort of information. Here are three key indicators that indicate a fan.

- ★ **The regular customer.** If a customer comes into your store on a regular basis—every week or, even better, every day—he's obviously committed to you and your product for a particular reason. Even if your business is simply in close proximity to his home, so you're easy to get to, you want to be aware of it. However, usually anyone who frequents your business on a regular basis is honestly just into your goods and services.
- ★ **The talkative customer.** When a customer stops to chat with your staff and takes a sincere interest in your product and your methods of operation, there is a good chance that she's a fan of what you do. If people are ambivalent about what you are doing, they won't be spending time chatting and asking question about your product.
- ★ **The complimentary customer.** If a customer is always telling you how much he likes what you do, or, even better, if someone else says to you, "So-and-so is always talking about your store, so we had to come check it out," you've found another fan of your establishment.

This is not rocket science, but it's a great guideline to jump-start your data tracking. If your customer does one of those three things, you absolutely must know more about her. No matter what business you are in, you have fans, and once you begin to identify who they are and their level of enthusiasm, you can implement tactics to grow their avidity and transform them into core fans who will be with you for a lifetime of purchases. It's important to remember that when consumers are fans, they do not mind paying if there is true value in what you offer *and* if you are making them feel special. Converting customers into fans is all about treating them the way they want to be treated.

So, if your first objective is to identify your fans, having the ability to capture and track their information must follow. If you have a mega database that can track a consumer's spending habits and likes, the way credit card companies do, you can be much more scientific in the process. If you're a small business and you do not have a plush database system (or even if you're a huge corporation but simply haven't started yet), don't sweat it. It's time to begin gathering information on your customers with the intention of understanding their avidity toward your brand. Yes, you have to invest time entering names and preferences into a database—no matter how basic it may be. I don't care whether you are a pizza joint or a huge financial institution, *you must* capture, gather, and utilize information about your consumers.

I don't mean "get their names and start spamming them with e-mails and promos." This is a totally different perspective.

THE RINGS OF FAN AVIDITY

Before we even begin, you must understand that when you're categorizing fans, you're not categorizing them by how much they spend with you. This is all about categorizing your fans by how much they love your brand so that you can work on making them love you more. When I worked in the radio industry, we categorized our listeners in a four-ring hierarchy to better understand who they were and how to increase the amount of time they spent listening. We grouped those listeners according to a pretty classic system from the radio industry, as P1s through P4s.

P1s (P1 stands for "First Preference" in the industry) were the core listeners to the station. They listened religiously, tuning in every day for many hours. They passionately followed the hosts and events affiliated with the station and demonstrated a strong avidity for the brand. P1s felt as though they were a part of the station and listening was personal for them; they were the kind of listeners who would classify the station as "theirs" and were completely loyal, often making plans around the station's schedule. The true goal of any radio marketer is to make everyone who listens to the station a P1 listener.

Just outside that inner ring were the P2s: regular listeners who tuned in multiple times per week to listen to several different daytime broadcasts. They enjoyed the station and what it had to offer, but P2s were never "all in" the way the core P1 listeners were. Instead, P2s would listen to the station, but would also sample other formats from time to time. Nonetheless, we were the P2s' favorite station and we knew they listened to us more than they did to any other station.

Moving further out from the inner ring, P3s were still frequent listeners, but they tended to tune in primarily once a week for a particular show. They might have tuned in a couple of times per week had it fit into their schedules, but that time commitment was completely on their terms and not dictated by their affinity for the station. P3s liked the station, but in comparison to the P1s and P2s, they were basic listeners with no real emotional connection to our brand.

Finally, P4s were infrequent listeners. They would tune in once in a while, but only if there was a specific reason driving them to listen. For example, P4s would most likely tune in to the station to get more information on a current sports story that was prevalent in the news, as they knew they'd be most likely to get that info from us. They knew who we were, but we weren't a part of their lives.

It was easy for me to transfer this four-ring categorization system to the Patriots, but it's important to know that this concept works for any company. Consumers of everything from caviar to tractors can be easily grouped into these categories. At the New England Patriots, we used the system to develop loyalty marketing programs and a customer service database system. If you want to *increase* avidity, you first have to know where it stands.

Moving Fans to the Inner Rings

The overlying concept of the four-ring fan categorization system is to take each tier and create mechanisms that move the people in it closer to the center. The goal of any marketer is to make P4s into P3s, P3s into P2s, and P2s into your core fan base, your P1s. Having a great product lays the groundwork, but other vehicles must be created to support and enhance fan avidity for long-term sustainability and growth. The focus here should be on identifying the characteristics of each ring and marketing to the *commonality* of each kind of fan instead of identifying individual preferences. Grouping fans into affinity rings will allow an organization to market directly to a particular group, thus strengthening and growing the fan base.

Make no mistake: your consumers are not all the same because they buy your product. As you build your database of customers, use your knowledge of them and your product to fit them into one of the rings. At the radio station, we based it on time spent listening. For a restaurant, it may be how many times a week the particular patron dines at your establishment. If you're a boutique marketing agency, it could be how many times each week your client calls with questions that are outside the scope of your services. Fans need to have interaction with your products and services. You should base your categorization of each client on the levels of both interaction and purchasing that are appropriate for your brand and your company. If you own a bakery, the group of customers that buy bread multiple times a week, get pizza every Saturday, buy pies on Mondays and pastries on Fridays, and only purchase their baked goods from your shop are most likely falling into the P1 ring, while the customer who buys a pie once in a while is a P4. Know who they are, collect their names and information, put them in your database, and categorize them into one of the rings.

Once you have a running database, you next need to understand what characterizes each group in order to create ways to increase people's avidity. Remember, the goal is to move people from ring to ring to ring, toward that P1 status. To do this, you must reach out and interact with each segmented group. Questionnaires and surveys are one mechanism to learn more about and define each group. SurveyMonkey is a spectacular tool for every company, large or small. If you are a bakery, give your customers an incentive to provide you with information; this free treat is a cost that you need to absorb if you are to grow your business. It's *as important* as advertising, Web site development, and a fancy new sign on the side of your shop. In fact, it may be even *more* important, because this information is the power that will fuel your efforts to achieve organic revenue growth.

PROMOTIONS THAT MOVE PEOPLE THROUGH THE RINGS

Once your entire database of customers has been subdivided, you'll want to create programs, promotions, opportunities, and exclusive offers specifically designed for each fan type. The objective of these promotions is to facilitate the fans' investment—both emotional *and* fiscal—in your company. The goal is to condition fans to connect with you, which then moves them toward the inner circle. Let's talk about the most classic example of programs designed to increase fans: loyalty programs. Well-developed loyalty programs have been proven to advance fans from the outer rings into the P1 category effectively; that's why you see them everywhere. Be careful, though. The main weakness of many of these programs is that they focus purely on higher levels of revenue, so many of them are really just mechanisms to convince people to buy more. Getting someone to buy more from you doesn't necessarily increase her avidity. Don't focus on the money during this part of the process. We'll get to that later.

Here, you're working toward the long-term sustainability of a customer relationship, so information and data should be viewed as capital, not just cash. Give rewards not only for spending and frequency, but also for data.

Consumer avidity programs have taken many different forms over the years. Airline frequent flyer programs have stood the test of time because they are easy to understand: Fly 10,000 miles and get a free upgrade. Fly 25,000 miles and get a free companion ticket with the purchase of a full-price ticket. Fly 50,000 miles and get a free ticket. At certain "promotional times," you can get double miles, provide information and get 10,000 miles, or sign up for an airline credit card and get 20,000 miles, which are all mechanisms to compel the consumer to think about frequency and volume with a particular airline. Credit card companies utilize similar point systems based on purchases to reward their consumers, but their points can buy a wide range of goods and services—even airline tickets.

The specific mechanism you choose to drive fan loyalty really does not matter. Rather, the key is to understand the fans of your company and their consumption habits in order to create vehicles that increase avidity and spending. Provide fans with a reason to make the leap to the next most inner avidity ring and continuously reinforce to them why they made that fan commitment in the first place—it's your responsibility to maintain and solidify their loyalty. This approach must be constant and fluid in order to be successful. In other words, this is not a "one and done" thing. The need to continually evolve and develop new, fresh ideas is crucial; lack of evolution is the reason that "fan clubs" fail. Many sports teams create fan clubs to foster this growth, yet the majority fall short and actually create more issues than goodwill with fans because there is no substance to the club. Whatever the program, there must be true value for the fan and the ability to receive more from your brand with the increase of fans' purchase frequency and information transfer.

Simple, Creative, and Dominating

Loyalty programs are only one mechanism to increase frequency and spending. Creative promotions are also effective in driving consumers to buy more product more often. This is not a revelation, but knowing that you have to create promotions to drive traffic and actually developing a creative, effective promotion are two very different things. We are not here to tell you what will work best for your consumers, but we are here to show you the proper ingredients for creating a successful promotion. When you're drawing up the ultimate promotion aimed at turning your consumers into fans, driving traffic, *and* generating revenue, your promotion must pass the SCD test. When I was in radio at the very beginning of my marketing career, my boss at the time, John Maguire, would ask me three questions every time I was about to introduce a new promotional concept. Almost 20 years later, I still use those questions to test the quality of my ideas every time I create something new.

★ Is the promotion *Simple?*
★ Is the promotion *Creative?*
★ Is the promotion *Dominating?*

In *The Tipping Point,* Malcolm Gladwell talks about making something memorable and, specifically, "stickiness." When you create promotions, you're specifically developing them to have that stickiness, so that people understand what the promotion offers and it grabs their attention. Think about all the products that you see being promoted every day of the week. The best "this"! The most amazing "that"! Buy "this," get "that," and we'll even throw in this brand new Cadillac. We are constantly inundated with information: in the street by billboards and radio and at home by television, the Internet, and smartphones. We are bombarded with information, and it's all businesses hoping to get consumers to pay attention. "Here I am! Here I am!" They're all screaming and yelling, and it's getting louder and louder.

It's become so loud that you can't hear anything.

When you create a mechanism that allows you to push through the clutter and stand out in the crowd, that's powerful. It makes a huge difference, no matter what product or brand you are marketing. Think about those promotions you've seen that have stuck in your mind—really caught your attention. Living in Boston, I'm exposed to many local promotions, and normally "local" means it's not as sophisticated or as effective as "national," but back in 2004, a local furniture store, Jordan's Furniture, hit one out of the park. Jordan's partnered with the Boston Red Sox, a historic franchise known at the time for not having won a World Series since 1918. The premise of the promotion was that everyone who bought furniture during a specific time frame at the beginning of the baseball season would win the furniture they purchased if the Red Sox won the World Series.

You couldn't go into a bar or hang out by the watercooler anywhere in Massachusetts and not hear people talking about the possibility of the Red Sox winning the World Series and finally breaking "the curse," so Jordan's capitalizing on that at the commencement of a new season was not only timely but also pertinent. If you happened to be buying furniture during that time period, it provided just cause for you to shop at Jordan's Furniture rather than another retailer—and the concept did drive business to Jordan's. The advertising and marketing initiative surrounding the promotion was focused and well executed, which caused the promotion to be a huge success. But it doesn't stop there: the Red Sox actually *did* win the World Series that year, and through it all, Jordan's message was that it wanted the Sox to win and it wanted to give away all that furniture *because the people at Jordan's were fans too*. Brilliant. The store built a simple, creative, and dominating promotion that had the ultimate payoff.

Simple   As you create promotions, you want to mimic what Jordan's Furniture accomplished. To do so, you need to ask yourself certain questions about the quality of the promotion you're developing. The Simple, Creative, Dominating test helps you determine if you have created an exceptional vehicle to move your consumer. Is the promotion simple? Is it easy to understand? Is it easy to participate in? If you get too complicated in a promotion, you're going to lose people—and you don't want to lose a lot of potential customers. For the most part, people are basically lazy, right? They're lazy, and they're not going to want to participate in a promotion that makes them jump through hoops. The Jordan's Furniture promotion was exactly that: buy stuff during this time frame and get it free if the Red Sox win the World Series. Pretty easy—even if you're lazy.

The Jordan's Furniture Red Sox promotion was also easy to execute for both the consumer and the contest administrator. When the Red Sox won the World Series, the insurance company paid off the claims on Jordan's behalf. (Jordan's had hedged its expenses by working with an insurance company in case the Red Sox *did* win and it had to reimburse its customers.) All Jordan's did was cut checks to reimburse customers who had bought furniture during the specified time frame. It was a detail-oriented process, but overall it was very manageable, and it was easy for Jordan's to keep its part of the bargain and keep customers happy. In fact, it went so well that Jordan's ran the promotion again.

Creative The second part of the promotional equation is creativity. Does your promotion stand out in the crowd? Does it overcome the clutter? There's all this crap being thrown at consumers every single day; does your idea separate your brand from the barrage? Is it memorable? For a promotion to qualify as truly creative, you need an unequivocal "yes" in response to all these questions. The Jordan's promotion was very creative, because it capitalized on a ubiquitous conversation in the Boston area: "When will the Red Sox finally break the curse and win the World Series?" The feeling was that the new Sox ownership was doing the right thing, filling the roster with players that would get us there. The optimism about the Red Sox was growing, and the timing was perfect to associate with the Sox brand and winning it all. Jordan's and its agency also did great creative messaging to support the concept.

Dominating The final piece of the test is its power to dominate the customer's attention. Is the promotion so compelling that it gets consumers to take action? Next, does it go beyond compelling—is it *everywhere?* That's where you find that "wow" factor: not only in the number of ads and vehicles promoting it, but also in the overall feel and perception of the promotion. Jordan's Furniture had that "wow" factor and was dominating not only because of the media support it put behind the promotion, but because it offered a real prize for something that every person in Massachusetts had been yearning for: the Red Sox winning the World Series. The power was that everyone was in this together, rooting for victory, and everyone who participated would win alongside the team. Jordan's was brilliant to tap into that emotion and provide another layer to the excitement.

The promotion was so simple, creative, and dominating that it made it hard not to pay attention to it, especially if you were in the market to buy new furniture. Think about it: if you had to buy furniture anyway and there was a convenient Jordan's Furniture near you, why wouldn't you shop there? In fact, I would guess that the promotion probably motivated customers to drive a little further. Jordan's is a reputable company, it carries high-quality products, and its prices are reasonable. Furniture shoppers had nothing to lose if they were planning to buy furniture anyway.

When you hit all three and create a simple, creative, and dominating promotion, even your staunchest critics will stand up and take notice. They may even quietly applaud your efforts. I'm sure all the other furniture stores in the Boston area were kicking themselves, wishing that they'd thought of the promotion before Jordan's did.

Simple, creative, and dominating is not some spectacular equation filled with marketing jargon. It's simply real and effective. Most marketers think *complicated* means *better*—the more whacked out a concept, the more off the wall, the better the promotion. So many companies create promotions that have multiple layers and all these bells and whistles and, because these promotions sound cool and complex, think they've come up with something great. Huge companies do this all the time: they want to be so different that no one can understand what the promotion is all about.

Complicated does not equal creative. You never want your participants jumping through hoops. I remember reading about a Wendy's promotion a few years ago in which it was giving away 10,000 Twisted Frostys, with one person winning a year's supply. Contestants could enter only on Wendy's Web site and were forced to go through four screens that required them to provide detailed information *and* fill out a survey about Wendy's. Once that was complete, they could play a game, and *if* the participant won, she would win a free Frosty and a chance to win Frostys for a year. That was a *lot* of steps to take to potentially win a $1 item with an outside chance of winning the not-so-grand prize.

In this case, I think the folks at Wendy's lost sight of what they were trying to accomplish. This really wasn't a promotion at all, and it *definitely* wasn't a mechanism to drive customers into Wendy's restaurants. It sounds as if the marketers at Wendy's wanted to gather information about their consumers or potential consumers while introducing the Twisted Frosty. Gathering information about your consumers is crucial, but Wendy's could have gathered the info it was after far more easily. For the price point of a small Frosty, Wendy's should have been true to the purpose of its efforts: it should have encouraged people to fill out detailed surveys and e-mailed every household that did so a small Frosty coupon. This approach would have gotten the company the information it wanted *and* driven customers to stores. This promotion's design shows upside all around: not only are you gathering information, but you're also driving folks to stores to spend.

Let's switch our attention to another fast-food chain. McDonald's is successful with its Monopoly promotion because, even though it's intricate, it works because almost everyone has played the Monopoly board game. Everyone already knows the rules, even though they're somewhat complex. That makes it simple and easy to understand, and, unlike the Wendy's promotion, McDonald's Monopoly actually drives consumers to McDonald's. Frequency is required to get matching properties, which you have to have if you want to win. Even when a participant doesn't get a property or a winning prize, he still gets a Coke or an order of fries, which entices many people to come back to redeem. It's a very well-thought-out promotion that meets the SCD test—and it's successful. That's why McDonald's does it year in and year out.

Little Bit of Time, Big Impact

With anything in media, you have only a short period of time to say a lot. With all the clutter flying by your consumer, you have to make your message stick. I have to tell you about the promotion I created with the Patriots that I believe, like the Jordan's Furniture promotion, met the SCD test. Interestingly, this promotion never actually took place. After we won our first Super Bowl, I was eating out of a box of Cracker Jacks, and the concept just popped into my head. Every time I eat Cracker Jacks, I always remember as a kid the thrill of opening up the box and wanting desperately to get to the prize inside before I ate a single kernel or nut. The excitement was real, even for a prize that was typically a little plastic ring. Eureka! How perfect! Why wouldn't we do a deal with Cracker Jacks and have a Patriots Super Bowl ring inside one of the boxes? What Patriots fan wouldn't go out to buy a box or two of Cracker Jacks in search of a coveted Super Bowl ring? This had all the makings of a simple, creative, and dominating promotion. No doubt this was a winner.

You want to know why it didn't happen? After much debate, we decided that we didn't want to commercialize the Super Bowl ring. It was a little disappointing, since it was such a perfect idea, but keeping the ring special was just a little bit better idea. I hope a company reading this goes out and makes that promotion a reality with its own brand—maybe we'll see Ford put a key to a new car in a box of Cracker Jacks.

PROMOTIONS FOR DIFFERENT Ps

The interesting thing about promotions like these is that, as memorable as they are, they're not directed at any one group. They're likely to increase the avidity of all your customers, a much more broad-stroke approach to turning customers into fans. Promotions at that scale are entirely inaccessible for smaller businesses, so whether you are a large or a small business, you have to explore other methods to grow your P4s to P1s. The key to this is the information you collect on each ring. Let's take the P2 ring as an example.

P2s are your best opportunity for conversion. These are people who have displayed affection for your product or service but who do not use your company exclusively. There are reasons why they are not committed to your organization the way P1s are committed. It's like you're dating each other and they like you best, but something is preventing them from jumping in head over heels. You may have done nothing wrong, by the way; it's just that you're missing something. Becoming more personal with the people in this group will help you detect what will sway them into the inner ring.

The best way to move P2s into the inner P1 circle is to find a mechanism that makes them feel special, as if they are your most important customers. Small businesses take notice, because this will be easier for you to accomplish than for bigger corporations. Big corporations have to simulate personal relationships with their consumers, but you can create an authentically personal relationship.

While everything you do causes the P1s to stand up and applaud, you need to work harder to move the P2s. This may sound inverted, but you ultimately have to treat your P2s even *better* than you treat your P1s. Face facts: you own the P1s. The likelihood is that they will be with you for the long haul. I'm not telling you to ignore your P1s—you have to maintain that relationship—but they're already "all in." To grow your business, you need to focus on the best *potential*, and that lies with your P2s.

EXTRA POINTS
In the next chapter, we will get back to P1s because,
although you may have *all* their avidity, you may not be tapping
into their entire potential spending with your company.
Don't confuse *avidity* and *spending*.

Shock and Awe

You need a bit of "shock and awe" to move the P2s. You have to create an offer or event that makes them stand up and take notice, one where they ask themselves two key things: "Do I deserve this?" and "How cool was it that I was invited to this?" The ideal promotion will evoke *both* a little unworthiness and a little exclusivity. Eliciting the pair of emotions means powerful positioning of your brand.

Create an exclusive opportunity that associates the P2s with your organization. It must clearly be extended to a limited number of people, and—this is important—it's always more high-impact when what you're offering cannot be purchased by the average consumer. Think about those cool experiential packages, like playing catch with Tom Brady or a private cooking lesson with Mario Batali; when those opportunities come up at auctions, people with discretionary cash jump all over them. Imagine being the person who invites people to stuff like that and the points you score with your clients.

When TrinityOne Marketing first opened its doors, we signed a deal with NASCAR's Richard Childress Racing. We took many big potential sponsors, like people from Staples and Ocean Spray, to races. But we didn't just hang out in the stands; we took them down into the pits, to meet-and-greets with drivers and Richard himself, gave them photo ops and great food—all the bells and whistles. The big clients, although appreciative, were more used to that kind of atmosphere and catering, but the smaller potential clients were always enthusiastic and amazed by these kinds of opportunities. Frequently they began proactively looking for ways to continue engaging with us, hoping to find ways to do business with RCR and TrinityOne—that's moving a client from P2 to P1.

If you're not a sports franchise, you have the same ability to migrate your P2s into the core of the rings of fan avidity by utilizing your assets or your connections to make P2s feel special. My buddy and restaurateur Angelo Caruso has a wine cellar in the basement of his restaurant, Angelo's. He and his dad, Sal, designed it in such a way that it's not just a cellar but a small, nicely decorated event space with a big table in the middle that displays some wonderful cheeses and Italian cold cuts. Angelo and Sal will walk selected people downstairs before sitting them down for dinner, chatting with their guests about food and wine while sharing nibbles of cheese or an excellent Chianti. They're not doing this only for big-name athletes or celebrities; their objective is to make frequent visitors to their restaurant feel that much more welcome and at home. This typifies engaging P2s with yourself, your brand, and your services. The feeling one gets when Angelo walks over and says, "Come with us," and Sal whispers, "This is only for the special people," is powerful.

FINAL THOUGHTS

No matter what type of company you run, you can offer something special to customers that will compel people to think of you, frequent your establishment more often, and evolve into true fans. If you own a bakery, perhaps you can invite them to an exclusive baking day and teach them how to make your bread recipe. Whatever it is, your promotions must be developed for no reason other than to increase avidity. Tap into it and begin making P1s out of your P2s.

What it comes down to is, as a company, you have to form relationships with your consumers so that you can understand them and offer them what they want. It's so simple: the more you know about them and the more you understand their likes and dislikes, the more you can cater to them. First and foremost, put in place the structure and mechanisms necessary to capture the information and act on it. Once you know who your consumers *really* are and where they fit within your organization, you will understand how to get them to spend more money and provide a lifetime of purchases. That's what we'll be looking at next.

BUILDING REVENUE-GENERATING EXTENSIONS

I was sitting in a construction trailer—the temporary marketing offices for the New England Patriots—wedged between Foxboro Stadium and a cement skeleton that would eventually grow into what everyone now knows as Gillette Stadium. One of the premium seating sales reps was coming off a tour of the new stadium with what I understood to be prospective club seat buyers. As the prospects got out of the golf cart, my jaw dropped. I was expecting suits, ties, and wingtips, but no! One of the dudes was wearing a Tedy Bruschi number 54 jersey and a baseball cap. They shook hands with the director of premium seating, David Pearlstein, and I headed out of the trailer to chat with him after they'd left.

I cornered David in the parking lot and started jumping all over him. "David, what the hell is going on here? You can't be taking fans on tours right now! Why would you waste time with regular fans—they'll never be able to afford club seats?" At that time, club seats were priced at $3,750, $4,750, and $6,000 per seat with a minimum of a 10-year commitment. David dug in his heels and insisted that these were "real" prospects, but I wanted no part of the explanation. I couldn't fathom that this was true.

I was wrong—and I probably should say "sorry" here, David.

I grew up in East Boston in a blue-collar family. My grandfather was a laborer, and there was no way that he could have ever afforded club seats, and so there I was, equating blue-collar industries with shallow pockets. But as someone who'd grown beyond that lifestyle and limited means, I of all people should have known better than to judge a book by its cover. These men sporting jerseys may have been blue-collar "regular" season ticket holders, but there was nothing regular about them. David's guests were business owners—contractors, plumbers, and landscapers—*not* the guys who were getting paid by the hour. Anyone who has ever received a bill from a plumber or a contractor knows they make some serious dough.

Needless to say, these were exactly the people we should have been targeting to purchase club seats: passionate fans who owned businesses and had plenty of discretionary cash. They were the perfect people to target to buy premium seats. How could I have missed it?

When we began marketing premium seats, I was completely focused on the price point rather than on defining the characteristics of the perfect candidate for club seats. Guess what? I'm not the only one who missed the point. Every day, folks who work in companies large and small across industries are leaving revenue on the table because they are looking at sales the same way. Folks are looking at the customer based on the surface-level target demographics instead of the deep reality of what those customers are about and where they will dedicate their discretionary cash. Media buyers do this all the time, and it makes me crazy. They slot their products in a category like adults ages 25 to 54 or men ages 35 to 54. Sure, this narrows the overall consumer universe down so that the advertiser feels like it isn't advertising to everyone, but are those labels really nailing your consumer with a precise dart? Companies small and large need to work to better identify their potential consumers.

In the case of club members, the key identifier turned out not to be the household income, but instead the level of affinity with the team. So, while finding potential customers who had the discretionary dollars to spend was part of the equation, if a consumer's sense of connection with the team was low, the likelihood of his spending money on a specialty item like club seats was slim. "Men ages 35 to 65 with a household income of $100K+" was giving us an incomplete picture. The key to getting close to closing business is finding each element of the full equation: target demo + affinity = real prospect.

Let's talk about what we figured out at the Patriots that can help you sort through your own customers and build stronger relationships with them so they'll spend more with your company.

THE THREE-TIER CUSTOMER MODEL

We have to start with one simple reality that everyone seemingly forgets: your customers are not all the same. Regardless of what business you are in, whether you've noticed it yet or not, your company has multiple levels—or different kinds—of customers, and they all want to be treated in different ways. If you don't treat each customer appropriately, you lessen the likelihood that that customer will spend as much as she's willing to. In short, if you treat everyone the same, you leave revenue on the table.

The best way to begin to treat customers most appropriately is to start treating them the way *they* want to be treated, not the way *you* instinctively want to treat them. Treating customers the way they want to be treated is the only way to maximize revenue, and you're going to do that by subdividing your existing customers based on their defining characteristics. Let me say at the outset that you can use any factor you like to start splitting customers into groups; you can define them by what they like, how much income they have, where they live, or anything else that illustrates who they are and what they want. It's easy to go pretty crazy and slice your customers into dozens of tiers (number of kids, propensity for travel, where they went to school, shoe size, and so on), but before you go nuts, I strongly recommend beginning with three simple tiers.

Getting Started: Organizing Your Tiers

Essentially, putting a customer into a "tier" is a way of identifying and labeling that customer as one who will spend money in a specific way. Creating tiers is much more than merely identifying who your customers are; it's about finding your fans and maximizing their opportunities to spend money with you in the ways they most want to spend it. Again, this is different from their level of affinity; in this chapter we're talking specifically about identifying and maximizing spending.

First, let's look at how to start identifying and assigning tiers. Initially, most companies view their consumers as one lump, the "customers." The very first, most obvious distinction you need to make—and this may not apply to all of you—is between those customers who are private consumers and those who are business-to-business clients. First, let's zero in on the private consumers. These are the people who make up your first tier, and it's important to recognize that 80 percent of the time, they're spending their own money. At the Patriots, this group would include the season ticket holders as well as people who occasionally buy tickets to games and merchandise.

That's what we're going to call our first tier: the *Season Ticket Holders Tier*.

The First Tier: Your Season Ticket Holders

Back in the late 1990s, when the New England Patriots played in Foxboro Stadium, the team had become so popular that every game was selling out. This means that it had found itself with more than 50,000 season ticket holders. It's key to understand that season tickets for an NFL team are not very expensive compared to those for other professional teams; there are 10 home games, and season tickets range in price from $450 to $1,000 a ticket per season. So, from a marketing standpoint, that's a nice chunk of change, but we viewed this entire group of customers as *merely* season ticket holders—they were the group who bought tickets and to whom we could occasionally sell some merchandise or get into $40 or $50 events, such as a draft party. Our thinking was that every now and then we could push these people on a larger-ticket item, but as far as we were concerned, it didn't go much beyond that. This was absolutely the wrong way to view our season ticket holders, because not only did they represent a significant amount of revenue for our organization, they also had the means to grow our revenue organically if we had approached them in the proper manner. You have to remember that these people are shelling out their hard-earned money to consume your product—and there are real reasons they do so.

Now, every company has a Season Ticket Holders Tier, but most companies probably don't look at them that way. Let's look at a higher-end restaurant, for example. A fine restaurant's Season Ticket Holders Tier are people who come to the restaurant often, maybe half a dozen times a year. They're good, solid customers that you can count on spending an average amount of money, and they collectively provide a solid, consistent stream of revenue for that restaurant. Season Ticket Holders

Tier customers are your bread and butter. You want to treat them right and provide them with great customer service. Because of the sheer number of them, while their individual spending might be modest, they represent a big chunk of revenue for your company. Don't take them for granted; they also represent your upside.

The Third Tier: The Corporate Sponsors

On the other end of the spectrum, your third-tier consumers are typically a limited number of individuals who spend significantly larger sums of money to accomplish goals that go far beyond having a great time on a Sunday afternoon at the game. They're usually business-to-business clients, people who are essentially spending other people's money. At the Patriots in the late 1990s, this top tier was made up of sponsors and suite holders; they're the people who buy team offerings like signage, logo rights, suites, and media. Take Dunkin' Donuts as an example. The rep from Dunkin' Donuts who is negotiating a deal with the team is typically in marketing himself and doesn't approach this kind of business transaction as though he were spending his own money. He is working on achieving the company's goals, but at the end of the day, he's spending other people's money, so he's a little less protective of it. Because the top tier is a much smaller group of clients, we as a marketing team know them as individuals, understand their likes and dislikes, and keep their specific goals in mind. This allows us to cater to their needs and customize a package of offerings that fits more precisely with their needs and desires.

So that we never forget the buying power and motivation of this tier, we're calling them the *Corporate Sponsors Tier*. To get back to our restaurant example, you can think of the Corporate Sponsors Tier as the companies that schedule large dinner parties, frequently entertain clients at the restaurant, and throw mini events in private rooms. If a restaurant's Season Ticket Holders Tier customer spends $100 at a meal, a Corporate Sponsor Tier customer spends $1,000+.

At this point, it should be clear that the Season Ticket Holders Tier and the Corporate Sponsors Tier represent the two ends of the spectrum. Now, no matter what size company you're running, even if you've never been involved in a business-to-business deal of any sort, you're still going to be able to pick out the third group, and they're the hidden jewels. This next group should represent significant untapped revenue for your company. Finding and cultivating this tier will help your margins dramatically, because, while you used to see these people as "just another season ticket holder," they belong in a tier all their own.

The Second Tier: Club Seats

So far we've talked about the everyday people, the Season Ticket Holders Tier, and the power players, your Corporate Sponsors Tier. However, it's in the middle tier, the group we're going to call *Club Seats Tier*, that you're going to find those people who are both serious fans of your business and game changers in your push to grow and generate revenue. While you're identifying this tier, you'll be extracting them from both the Season Ticket Holders Tier and the Corporate Sponsors Tier, but this is primarily about identifying and facilitating more spending from names that are buried in your long list in the Season Ticket Holders Tier.

You may realize already that I'm going to challenge you to rethink your database. We hear how important database marketing is all the time in business conversations: "Get *new* names! Get *new* e-mail addresses!" Yet the list of people that you already have is your most powerful resource for effective marketing because it identifies consumers who are already fans of your brand. Yet for some reason, most companies tend to spend more of their budget trying to gain new customers than they do to cultivate their current consumers. Think of it this way: imagine one of your most loyal customers calls you up to tell you that she just hit the lottery and that she wants your advice on how to spend some of the money—and by the way, one of the activities she enjoys most in life is using your products. That conversation is an engraved invitation for you to introduce her to more of your goods and services. Identifying members of your Club Seats Tier is all about finding and replicating that sort of opportunity.

Consider this: because of the relative affordability of getting into the Season Ticket Holder Tier, your list of names of individuals and families who have purchased your "season ticket" is, in a word, long. Because of the sheer magnitude of this list (for you it might be a list of everyone who has *ever* purchased a product or service from you), it's very difficult to parse out those people who have real money to spend and who have a real affinity for your product—which makes it hard to determine who's right for a particular promotion or product and who isn't. Without extracting the names of people who are ready to hear from you and, more important, are able to respond with their wallets, mass mailing to those lists is like throwing spaghetti against the wall to see what sticks. As a young marketer, I was certainly guilty of this approach.

The objective is to identify a more affluent group of people who have more discretionary dollars and *who you already know are fans of your team*. OK, I know it sounds simple, but all you are trying to do is to gather more detailed information about your current consumers so you understand who has additional discretionary dollars to spend and is prone to spend them with you. The answer to growing your revenue is right in front of you, and you're probably spending your budget on attracting new customers when you haven't even scratched the surface of the spending potential of your current consumers.

The funny part of this three-tier thinking is that it is something we stumbled on accidentally when we were building and moving to the new stadium. Here's the background of how it all developed, so you can use our experience to determine how to define your own Season Ticket Holders, Club Seats, and Corporate Sponsors Tiers.

INITIAL EFFORTS: HOW BUILDING A NEW STADIUM REVOLUTIONIZED OUR MARKETING

When I started with the Patriots, Foxboro Stadium was a lousy place to watch a game (the whole place was just bench seats), and we really had only two types of customers in our database. You guessed it: season ticket holders and corporate sponsors. That was basically it. Naturally, when we started to build the new stadium, we placed extreme focus on selling the 6,000 club seats first, as their sale was imperative for the financing of the stadium. At that point, we were confident that our season ticket holders would buy regular tickets and our corporate sponsors would purchase suites and other marketing inventory.

On top of the assumptions we made about the spending we'd see from our season ticket holders and corporate sponsors, we went a fairly traditional route with our initial marketing efforts. OK, I'll be honest: it was totally run of the mill. We grounded our marketing plan in chatting with the corporate community, reaching out to mailing lists that we purchased, and hoping that some folks on the season ticket waiting list would be candidates. We assumed we were looking for white-collar executives who liked to use entertainment to drive business—after all, they were the people with money to spend, right? We looked at lists of businesses and dug up corporations that might be likely to buy hospitality and entertainment experiences for their clients. Sure, we got a little traction from this plan, but not nearly as much as we would have liked.

The folks in charge of selling premium seating realized, obviously before I did, that current season ticket holders and people on the season ticket waiting list were real candidates for purchasing these high-priced memberships. As I mentioned at the beginning of the chapter, fans were literally coming down with their Bruschi jerseys wanting to secure club seats, and it made total sense: die-hard fans of the team were a natural resource for increased revenue before the team had even produced truly exceptional results.

The mistake we made was that we completely underestimated our current customers. It's easy to fall into the trap of thinking that your regular customers spend a set amount of money, and, because that's all they have ever spent, that's all they can or will spend. It's this assumption that leads so many business owners and marketing managers to put all their time and money into finding new customers instead of investing their resources in cultivating their current customers. It's classic to continually look for new people to start eating at your restaurant instead of encouraging existing customers to attend a special wine pairing or chef's select dinner event.

Focusing on identifying the likes and purchasing patterns of your current customers is always more efficient for generating new revenue than searching for brand new customers.

EXTRA POINTS

Again: don't think for your customer. The likelihood is that you do not understand your customer's story until you ask him the right questions. In our case, it turned out that many of our season ticket holders were business owners who had plenty of discretionary dollars to spend and enjoyed the finer things in life but simply didn't have the VIP connections that it can take to get the special access that celebrities or dignitaries have. Once they held club seats, we became their conduit to that access and made them *feel* like they were celebrities. To be completely candid, it's in your best interest to target enthusiastic fans with large discretionary incomes *who need you to help them get access to special treatment that they might not otherwise receive.* They're the perfect targets of marketing efforts like these.

It ultimately turned out that those folks who qualified as real club seat material hadn't been spending up to their potential in the past because we weren't providing opportunities for them to spend. *Literally, we weren't asking them to spend money.* Why weren't we asking them to do so? *Because we didn't know they were there. We had no idea who they were!* Yes, we knew their names, but we had no true concept of their desire or their potential ability to spend more money with us.

One of the ultimate benefits of being a club member of an NFL team is access to Super Bowl tickets when that team wins the division championship. When lightning struck and the Patriots won the AFC Championship in 2001 and headed to the Super Bowl, our affluent season ticket holders and many people on the season ticket waitlist realized that they could get tickets to the Super Bowl by purchasing premium seating. We were able to capitalize on the AFC Championship to sell club seat memberships and get closer to the 2,000 members we needed to be completely sold out (6,000 club seats with an average of 3 per member). Now, 2,000 may not sound like that many people when the season ticket holder list is 50,000 strong, but as an organization, we suddenly had an identifiable group who altogether spent around $20 million on club seats. They were now the source of a spectacular new revenue stream beyond the price of admission.

Never Close the Opportunity for Further Revenue

Once those season ticket holders upgraded themselves to club seats status, we now had this group of people we knew by name who were a major source of revenue for the team. We could have left it at that, but we like to make mistakes only once; we made no assumptions about these individuals and their capacities to spend. Instead, we began to communicate with and cater to this group, searching for and recording information that we had never possessed before. We began creating more personal relationships with these individuals because the task was so much more manageable than doing so with all 50,000 customers lumped together.

We found out that certain folks enjoyed golfing, others enjoyed travel, and others liked family-friendly events. This information helped us to sell out golf tournaments, gala dinners, and other higher-price-tag events for which our original knee-jerk sales reaction would have been to ask corporate sponsor members first. The problem with corporate sponsors is that they tend to operate on fixed budgets, and at times they wanted these items included as part of their overall packages, anyway. The discretionary spending from that group could be limited at times. Besides, it would be a mistake to force new initiatives on corporate sponsors if it didn't fit with their strategy. With the club seats taking over the purchasing of the tickets to these events, we were able to go back to corporate sponsors for other higher-margin opportunities that better suited them. In addition, all this information led us to create additional team-centric events around the activities our customers liked. Ultimately, it wasn't a surprise that once we started designing spending opportunities around our customers' desires, whatever we asked those club seats members to do, they were more prone to do. These people loved both the team and the finer things, so they wanted to get in on any opportunity we could create for them. They *enjoyed* spending money with the team, and what club seats inadvertently did was create the opportunity for them to know where and when they could do just that.

Knowing more than the names of all the people who were spending with us allowed us to interact with them and build relationships with them at much deeper levels. We were able to take people who were buying two or three club seats and amplify their spending because they enjoyed their experience and couldn't get enough of the team and the special treatment. Some club members upgraded to suites, and others rose to sponsorship levels. The leaps they were taking and the multiplication of revenue was mind-boggling. The subdivision of our customers, coupled with the team's success on the field, was like lightning in a bottle. The amazing thing was that whether the club seat member was in a white-collar or a blue-collar industry, each one wanted to feel special and enjoy the team-based experiences.

It's key to understand that it doesn't matter whether you're marketing for a team, a restaurant, or a bank; once you know who your customers are and you can subdivide them into tiers based on their preferences and spending levels, then you can organically and strategically grow your revenues. We now understood the people we classified as Club Seats Tier members. We knew what they wanted, so we could create any high-quality product or service driven by the brand, and their answer would always be yes. It was powerful marketing, fueled even further by the team's increasingly better performance on the field. But make no mistake: although the winning magnified the outcome, if we hadn't identified the candidates for these bigger-ticket opportunities, we would have generated significantly less revenue, regardless of the wins. Many teams have won Super Bowls and built new stadiums without experiencing the revenue growth we had at the New England Patriots.

The hardest element of business is identifying and understanding those consumers, sponsors, and partners who will spend two hundred thousand to a million dollars with you. It's easy to find the people who are going to spend a couple of thousand—they come out of the woodwork. But finding those individuals who are going to spend significant amounts with you, people who will "buy club seats," is tricky, and understanding the three-tier hierarchy is the best way we've found to do so.

Let's put our results in perspective: prior to building the new stadium, the Patriots Charitable Foundation luncheon produced about $50,000 in revenue. Once we identified the Club Seats Tier people, that number grew to close to $300,000. That's just one event, one snapshot of the business. Every ancillary effort we created generated revenue at multiples of what we would normally have expected had we not isolated this unique group of consumers. So why, then, do companies traditionally spend more of their budgets trying to recruit new customers instead of utilizing their resources to maximize the expenditures of the customers they already own? Winning the current customers cannot be overlooked; it's a revenue-building opportunity, not just a case of customer maintenance.

Identifying and Creating Tiers at Your Company

If I haven't already emphasized this enough, companies can almost never spend too much time looking at their current consumers. You do yourself and your bottom line a disservice when you look at all consumers the same way, so it's imperative that you spend time and money on your database, subdividing it and understanding who's who so that you can build dynamic revenue. If you're not already doing this, don't sweat it. You're in good company: to this day there are a surprising number of NFL teams that have one database for season tickets, another for marketing sponsors, another for people who buy merchandise, and another for people who buy the team newspaper. It's a nightmare: there could be someone who buys the team paper for $29 a year who is a millionaire—and you would have no idea. Or that person spending $29 could *already* be a sponsor, and you would *still* have no idea. It's safe to say across the board that even in sports, an industry where millions sit on the line every week, there's a huge disconnection of databases.

When I was at the team, we had a seven-figure client who also had a subscription to our team newspaper, *Patriots Football Weekly*. The only problem was that neither his account executive nor I knew about this. The client also happened to hold season tickets. Prior to the team's unifying its database, this seven-figure client was on three separate team databases and yet was completely under the radar on two of them. This was an absolute disaster waiting to happen. Nothing totally disastrous happened because we were lucky, but it's important to recognize the danger here: what if one week he didn't receive his issue of the newspaper, and he picked up the phone and called the subscription number for the paper? What kind of service would he get? The very idea leaves me petrified because I have no certainty about what would happen. The person handling subscriptions for a $29 purchase is probably not looking at this guy like he's a million-dollar client. I could pretend and say that everybody receives the same customer service regardless of her level of spending, but that's just not real.

Those databases left us in a precarious position. What if the person who answered the phone had had a bad day and treated our seven-figure client as if he spent only $29 with the team? Again, let me clarify: We want all our customers treated with the utmost care, but what if our client were treated like a nuisance and dismissed on the phone? I have to tell you: no one wants to receive the next call he would make.

Without a unified database, you are absolutely flying in the dark. Remember, everyone wants to be treated with respect, but the expectations of someone who buys a newspaper are very different from those of someone who is spending millions of dollars. The individual (and appropriate!) expectations of the customer need to be met during every interaction. How is that remotely possible if you do not know to whom you are talking?

This is not isolated to NFL teams or sports; this is true of companies all over. How do I know? At TrinityOne, we deal with clients and potential clients who have multiple databases and departments working in silos every day. Even when we do not work with them, it's easy to pick out the companies that do it right. Those companies stand out from the crowd because they are so few and far between. Credit card companies absolutely get it. American Express does a great job with this; it's blatantly obvious with just the colors of its cards. It subdivides Green, Gold, Platinum, and Black based on spending. The more it slices up the consumer list, the easier it is for the company to identify and track its customers' likes and dislikes. That way, it is able to match the perfect promotion or product to each customer.

As a business owner, you must make sure that you have someone in charge of your database—and that's not the person in your tech department! You need a real marketing person running the database. Remember, this isn't about keeping a list so that you can market an event or some sale; it's about developing a comprehensive portrait of your clients that allows you to create opportunities *for* them. Too many people think about marketing as, "We've decided we're going to do this event because we think people should like it. Write up the e-mail and send it out to the database." With that type of e-mail, it's easy to understand why 90 percent of the people don't even open the message. They're thinking, "What the heck does this have to do with me?" Sure, you might get some sales from that type of play—we know it generates at least enough sales to perpetuate this way of doing business as the norm. But throwing spaghetti at the wall is no way to run a business, regardless of the industry you are in, and it's certainly not the way to maximize revenue and organic growth.

The Birth of the Revenue-Generating Extension

Using the three-tier customer model, we learned to look at it like this: "OK, we have these people in the Club Seats Tier. They all are big fans of our team, they have discretionary dollars, they all own more than one home, they all drive a particular type of car, and so on. What types of things involving the Patriots would they like to see created that will make them drop money?" Just knowing who they were wasn't enough; we needed to know more about them. What were their preferences? Where did they shop? We were on a perpetual hunt for every detail—we were committed to getting into these people's heads and understanding their ways of thinking. Once we knew these things, it provided us with the ability to give them what *they* wanted, *not sell them what we wanted*. The former is a much easier way to accomplish your marketing goals.

Depending on the size of your customer list, there are several ways to go about getting to know them better. Now, if the group you're looking to get info from is large, like 50,000 people, you're going to have to create a mechanism that compels people to fill out a survey. There's just no other way to get this kind of information from throngs of people. So, for example, if you are a restaurateur, you go to your Season Ticket Holders Tier with a survey and say, "You'll receive a free dessert or after-dinner drink for filling out this survey, and you'll also be entered for an opportunity to win a special wine dinner for four." You are enticing them to provide the information you need to build and subdivide your database.

Believe it or not, at one time we didn't have many e-mail addresses for our season ticket holders. We sent a note to all our season ticket holders saying that if they provided their e-mail address, they would be entered in a contest to win an autographed Drew Bledsoe jersey. That was enough motivation for a large number of the season ticket holders to provide that information. No one knows your company and the industry you are in better than you do, so you need to use your judgment and determine what item or perk will elicit the response you are looking for. Perhaps the offer is something like an e-book, a seminar, a gift certificate, or some other prize that people will *actually want*. You have to find something that's low- to no-cost to your company but has perceived value to your customers in exchange for something that costs *them* nothing other than a little time.

Now, of course, my advising you to use surveys isn't exactly groundbreaking advice, but again, when you're dealing with a large number of customers and you need to gather data, a survey's a solid method of gaining intelligence about your consumer.

Every time a club seats member contacted the Patriots for any reason (and now when any client calls TrinityOne), that call was logged and attached to the appropriate profile. We're not the Department of Homeland Security, and we're not in the business of recording calls without consent, but we do specifically log the information we are able to mine from each call that is pertinent to understanding the customer. As someone gets off the line, notes from the call are put into the database: the date, the topic of the conversation and, most important, any information we were able to gather about that person during the call that can assist us in understanding what he is all about.

So, a file might show that John Smith called with a question about a particular game date, but he mentioned that he's traveling to play golf and that he's extremely passionate about his golf game. If you're really paying attention and carefully tagging your database files, you may notice eventually that you've got 40 or so Club Seats Tier members who love golf and haven't ever played Pebble Beach, but it's on their list of things to do before they take the eternal dirt nap. The new revenue-generating extension now might be a trip to the legendary Pebble Beach Golf Course with a few former players. For us, it also meant that we knew whom to call to quickly sell out our Patriots Charitable Golf Tournament.

A more recent way to get into the minds of your customers and learn more about them turns out to be incredibly economically feasible and efficient: social media. As you begin to connect on LinkedIn, Twitter, and Facebook, you'll actually find that personal and broad information is *inbound*; you rarely have to ask or go hunting for it. When you can engage folks and find out what they want in these passive arenas, you remove that feeling of being overbearing (no one likes to be hounded) and create a free arena for your prospects and connections to dole out information with no pressure. Just because you learn something about a particular customer on social media doesn't make that information any less valuable than what you discover from an official survey or in time-consuming one-on-one live conversations. As soon as you find out anything about the preferences of your customers, put it in the database!

EXTRA POINTS
For a sample database template and ideas on how to customize your database for your own company, check out http://louimbriano.com/winningthecustomer-reference.

Because we were constantly gathering this intelligence, we were able to create what I call revenue-generating extensions with our customers in mind. These "extensions" do exactly what they sound like: they *extend* opportunities for participation in team-related events and promotions (often in nontraditional ways) that engage fans while generating new revenue for the team. Designing these extensions became incredibly easy to do after we'd identified our tiers—in fact, marketing became that much more fun because we were able to take the guesswork out of the process of designing promotions. Why any company would choose to forgo these tools and insist on marketing the hard way—perpetually guessing at what their consumers would like to buy—is beyond me.

REVENUE-GENERATING EXTENSIONS

One of the strongest moves you can make when you begin to develop revenue-generating extensions, particularly for your Club Seats Tier, is to *design extensions using the business initiatives you already have in place.* Don't try to reinvent the wheel if you don't have to.

Let's look at a sports-specific example to clarify what I mean. Theoretically, any stadium could be built with 60,000 identical seats. The $125 seat at the 50-yard line could be completely identical to the $43 seat in the nosebleeds up in the 600 level. We've become so accustomed to stadiums *not* operating this way that it's easy to forget that the different values in seating are all *by design.* The most basic way in which teams can provide spending opportunities for customers with extra income (and, obviously, for their sponsors) is to optimize not just the location of the seat but the whole atmosphere at that location in the stadium. Providing wider seats that are cushioned and have more legroom, like first class in a plane, is a perfect way to begin developing those factors that justify spending additional dollars. The ones that really want to sell, though, take it much further and pile on the perks. They add in private parking, special lanes into the stadium, exclusive events, and a higher quality and larger selection of food and drink options. All of these additions to the premium seat area in the stadium take very little extra work, but they *feel* exponentially better to customers and, most important, create exponential revenue.

The beauty of this is that everyone can look at developing revenue-generating extensions for their own companies in the same way. You need to think about what you have to build on. What do you already offer in your standard business model that you can amplify with real *and perceived* value for your customers so that you can ask them to pay more for it? Remember that once you've identified those customers who can pay for more, you don't have to be afraid of asking them to do so. Not only do they not mind, they are usually enthusiastic about doing so. It's this one simple tool that gives you a great advantage over your competition in generating additional revenue.

The key to creating revenue-generating extensions is knowing how your consumer fits with your company. When I was with the New England Revolution (Major League Soccer), we were selling seats for as little as $10 a seat, and we were still not sold out. You have to sell a boatload of seats to make money at that price point and, quite frankly, Club Seats Tier members, as much as they loved the organization, didn't have strong interest in buying $10 seats. Knowing that they didn't mind spending money and that they enjoyed special access, we created a revenue-generating extension called the *Presidents Club*. The Presidents Club took all the characteristics that Club Seats Tier members enjoyed and delivered them through the soccer team.

The Presidents Club seats were pitch-side seating, like courtside seating in the NBA. Great season tickets to the Revolution cost just over $300 for the season, so we priced the Presidents Club at $1,000 per ticket for the season. In addition to sitting right in the midst of the action, Presidents Club members received a bunch of amenities, including watching warm-ups prior to the game, which always included players going over to sign autographs. With the Presidents Club, we created a mechanism for capturing an entirely different audience that enjoyed access and experience regardless of the sport. We nearly sold out the first year (200 seats) and found a new revenue stream that didn't erode any of our previous seating programs. That is exactly what you want in a revenue-generating extension.

When you begin creating revenue-generating extensions, make sure they have these three characteristics: (1) They have to include offerings that consumers actually want, but that are not traditionally part of what you are currently selling. (2) They have to include something that is special and unique that extends access, experience, and value. (3) Whatever you're doing must not erode or negatively affect traditional revenue streams. A new dish or menu item at your restaurant is not what we are talking about, but selling the naming of a booth or table that is available on request to the patron who purchased it *is*. That's a revenue-generating extension.

Don't Forget the Customer Service

While you're considering the kinds of perks you'll use to amp up what you already offer, you must remember that customer service is an integral part of every revenue-generating extension. Most CEOs fear additional actions that are not overtly supporting the bottom line; they tend to think those actions are purely an expense. Because of this, they commonly view the customer service department as a cost center for their company. What they overlook when they dismiss the utmost in customer service is that the majority of consumers will happily pay more for exceptional customer care: customers *love* the Four Seasons' level of attention. *Every* Club Seats Tier consumer knowingly pays more, without question, for that service and for special treatment. Don't be afraid to include the cost of truly exceptional customer service in the price; it increases your chances for recurring business.

When I was at the Patriots, one of my best customer service people was a gentleman named Bill Nelsen. Bill embodied customer service, and the premium seat members loved him. When they had a problem or a question, Bill was their first stop. Now, he didn't always have the answer they wanted to hear, but Bill held everyone's hand through the sales and service process and had an off-the-charts success rate in customer happiness. Bill's role was integral to our success because the model we operated in was based on relationships. We were committed to building revenue-based relationships with our consumers that were so solid that we were always who they thought of first when it came time to spend their discretionary dollars. Bill and our group made people want to come back and spend more.

I guarantee you that if most CFOs looked at what we paid Bill, compared it to his job description, and then compared it to the specific revenue that could be directly attributed to him, they would *explode*. Believe me, they would insist that we were overpaying him . . . and they would absolutely and emphatically be *wrong*. There is no equation for what Billy did, but if I had to guesstimate, I'd say he was responsible for at least 10 times his salary in indirect revenue generation. He also minimized the need for higher-level executives to address problems, which saved the organization money and time, affording us the time and opportunity to create even more revenue-generating extensions and mechanisms for the organization to generate more revenue.

★ CASE STUDY: THE PATRIOTS TEAM TRIP ★

One incredible revenue-generating extension that exploded at the Patriots was the opportunity for select consumers to participate in official team trips. As we talk about team trips, pay careful attention to all the ways we maximized revenue by enhancing business practices that we already had in place and think about how they parallel practices within your own company.

In the course of doing business, the team traveled to away games in other cities eight times in the regular season (more if you include the preseason and the playoffs). The team traveled as such a large group that we had to charter a plane for each trip in addition to arranging ground transportation, hotel accommodations, and meals. Before we built the new stadium, we would take a handful of sponsors on the team plane; when the team was moving 175 people already, adding 10 or so marketing guests did not add a major expense and wasn't heavy lifting. It was a nice little perk for our select sponsors, but it wasn't really utilized to the fullest.

When I went on my first trip, I was blown away at its pure power: it mesmerized our guests, and yet, quite honestly, there wasn't much to it. Guests went on the plane, we had dinner with them, they got on the field prior to the game, they saw the game, and we flew them home. To be fair, for most fans, that alone would be a dream come true. But after going on a few trips, I saw so much more potential and power in team travel: once you are moving that number of people, the cost and effort to add additional people is minimal.

Remember: you don't need to reinvent the wheel when you can expand on what you already have in place. Let's examine the reimagined Patriots Team Trip, and you can see for yourself how a little plane flight, dinner, and a game evolved into an incredible experience for our guests.

Soon after building the new stadium, we upgraded to a larger plane that allowed us 50 seats on every flight for marketing purposes. We jumped at the chance to maximize revenue on those seats and started looking beyond the sponsors who had trips in their contracts. We began inviting sponsorship prospects and, most important, Club Seats Tier members, who paid $10,000 a trip to join the fun. Once we had this captivated audience, we needed to utilize this experience to deliver the three key aspects of revenue-generating extensions while also utilizing it to build unbreakable business relationships.

The day before the game, we would meet Team Trip travelers at the stadium, where they were greeted with a welcome reception that included coffee and breakfast. Once everyone had arrived and it was time to get on our way, we would go through a private security screening at the stadium (this is even after the new FAA regulations resulting from 9/11) and boarded a bus that we had reserved exclusively for our guests, in addition to the four buses for coaches, players, football staff, and administration. The buses, led to the airport by a police escort, would all drive directly onto the tarmac; there, we would unload and climb the stairs to the plane. Coaches and executives were in first class, marketing guests were in business class, and the players were in coach. (I know what you're thinking: "Huge offensive linemen in coach? No way." Believe it. They sat with an empty seat between them, but they were in coach just the same.)

Aloft at 36,000 feet, a Patriots Team Trip was unlike any normal flight experience. First, the team nutritionist traveled with us—after all, we were feeding players the day before a big game. The food was over the top, and it kept coming and coming. We started off with nuts, trail mix, and snacks; got into some warm chicken fingers or fruit; and then had steak or pasta. Later there were more snacks, candy, and Häagen-Dazs bars; it was more food then even a football player could eat—and every guest ate like a player. Inevitably the guests mentioned the amount of food and the size of the players.

After landing, we would board a new set of buses that was waiting for us on the tarmac. A police escort took us to the hotel, where room keys waited in the lobby for everyone; of course, we'd already checked our guests into the hotel. They grabbed their keys and proceeded to a conference room, where Coach Belichick would give a little talk, answer some questions, and have a photo op with our guests.

EXTRA POINTS

I want to stop here for a minute because that meet and greet is the epitome of everything we think about when we develop revenue-generating extensions. That special-access element of the package makes it priceless. It basically took 15 minutes and zero additional expense, but it packed maximum impact. This restricted access takes a fun trip, makes it spectacular, and adds extreme value. When you add elements that cannot be purchased off the shelf to your revenue-generating extensions, you exponentially increase the perceived value. When the perceived value is greater then the real cost of the goods, you can charge more and increase your margins. Finding something priceless is a way to make sure you make money.

Surprises also awaited our guests in their rooms. There they discovered an overstuffed duffel bag that included Patriots shirts, hats, jackets, and other team paraphernalia. The message light on the room phone flashed red, signaling a voice mail. When our guests retrieved the message, they heard something like this: "Hi, this is Adam Vinatieri. Welcome to your Patriots Team Trip. We have a lot of fun in store for you while the team prepares for a victory against the Dolphins. Have a great time, and if you need anything during the trip, do not hesitate to reach out to a marketing representative. There's a list of numbers in the bag you found on the bed. Don't forget to be in the hotel lobby at 7 p.m. if you are joining the group for dinner. Have a great trip, and Go Pats!" This was also priceless. Remember, the more you add, the greater the experience and the perceived value, which lets you charge that much more for the experience.

All our guests met for dinner in a private room at a great local restaurant. But dinner didn't stop at eating and spending time together—as the marketing team, we were obsessed with making our guests feel like kings and queens. Again, because we kept these extremely detailed databases, we had serious info about their preferences: we considered it our job to know who liked steak, who preferred lobster, who drank wine, and who didn't drink—we made everyone feel loved and at home. Our database allowed us to say things like, "Doug, can I get you a Beck's?" rather than, "Can I get you a beer?" Everything was extremely personal—by design. I would stand up at the beginning of dinner and ask if I could order appetizers for the table. Thanks to the database, every diner was thrilled with the selection. The key is to make everyone feel special and comfortable at the same time.

When dinner was over, there were always two groups within our party: those who wanted to head back to the hotel and those who wanted to party all night long. We were prepared for both, and we had always designated ahead of time who on the staff would be responsible for each group. Again, the key was to have everyone feeling comfortable, regardless of whether he decided to rock or to snooze.

The next morning, we met at a specially planned breakfast at the hotel, then piled onto buses to head over to the stadium— where, to pump up the excitement, we entered the stadium as the team did and proceeded to the field. We hung around the field watching pregame warm-ups and chatting until an hour before the game, at which point the Patriots' owner, Robert Kraft, came to the field to say hello to everyone (*by name*, I should add) and take pictures with our guests. (Do I need to say, "Priceless"?) Of course, a snapshot wouldn't suffice; we inserted each guest's photo into a Patriots logo matte and sent it home to display along with a note thanking the guest for joining us.

Not only was the photo something that the guests cherished, but we as marketers also counted on it to serve as a constant reminder of a memorable moment with the team. After photos, we moved up to a suite or club seats to eat, drink, enjoy the game, and solidify the bonds of the great relationships we'd been fostering all weekend. After a game (and hopefully a victory), we met at the buses. I say hopefully because if we won, the players would sign autographs and chat with the guests; if we didn't, it was a little less fun. As you can imagine, there was a huge difference between a victory and a loss on the flight home.

The good news is that a loss never changed the bonds we had built in the 36 hours that we spent with our guests. We would head back home in the manner in which we arrived, and the results were always successful.

How operations and planning, relationship building, and generating revenue all play together is the essence of our philosophical approach. If you can employ all three flawlessly while you create revenue-generating extensions, not only will you generate revenue in the short term, you will also help solidify the customer relationship. You have created a self-fulfilling perpetual mechanism to ensure that you are consistently winning the customer.

★ CASE STUDY: VISA SIGNATURE ★

Remember how we mentioned American Express earlier as an obvious example of a company that segments its database effectively to design perfect revenue-generating extensions? Visa has similar strategies that go well beyond issuing differentiated physical cards. Naturally, Visa customers run the gamut as far as different levels and frequency of spending go. The program "Visa Signature" is Visa's version of club seats; like our Club Seats Tier, this Signature group is a more active group of spenders who have discretionary dollars. Visa marketers understand the consumers that they enroll in Signature and market to them in a very different way from other cardholders.

You have to understand this: even though these cardholders earn high incomes and have some dough to spend, they are not billionaires. They want to *live* like billionaires. Most people want to live the glamorous life and may have the wherewithal to do so, but they lack the connections to get special access to experiential events. Visa understands the psyche of these consumers and provides opportunities and access to events and experiences that can be paid for with a Visa card that feeds its customers' "Signature" needs. Visa Signature creates revenue-generating extensions that provide its members with access to a myriad of special opportunities that are not afforded to the masses or to regular Visa cardholders. For example, by joining Signature, cardholders can purchase tickets to events like the Olympics, the Tonys, or the Kentucky Derby through Visa. These types of events are right in the wheelhouse of Signature customers; whether or not they like bobsledding, the theater, or horse racing, this tier of consumers wants exceptional experiences, and Visa will provide one that fits their profile.

Let's take the Kentucky Derby for an example. The Derby is not just a two-minute horse race; it's an *über* event that captures what the Signature cardholders are all about. The pageantry, the "who's who" of athletes, and the celebrities swarming Millionaire's Row are perfect, and Visa is the conduit to this spectacle for Signature members. However, Visa doesn't stop the revenue-generating extension at simply getting its special members to the event. Visa marketing pros, led by Michael O'Hara Lynch, know how to package the entire event and make it unforgettable. They bring their customers into the paddock areas, give them tours of the stables, arrange special VIP breakfasts with experts in the sport, offer suites, and designate club areas; the experience defines the full treatment that most people would never experience if they did not have Signature cards.

Think about all the sponsorships that Visa acquires—the Super Bowl, the Olympics, the World Cup—do you see a trend? They're all once-in-a-lifetime events. If you're not going to them, you are watching them on TV and discussing them with your friends. While they may just seem like simple sponsorships to people who are watching at home, simple ads designed to capture the attention of the masses, Visa uses sponsorships and relationships that they'd already created to design revenue-generating extensions that provide the holders of the Signature card the opportunity to live beyond their stature in these memorable moments. Brilliant.

MAKING IT YOUR OWN

The beauty of revenue-generating extensions within a three-tier marketing customer model is that you don't have to be an NFL team or a global corporation to identify your tiers and utilize the power that knowing them provides. Any company, regardless of its size or number of customers, should be looking at its database, slicing it to get a more precise understanding of its consumers' ability to spend, and creating specific extensions for each tier.

★ CASE STUDY: ISIS PARENTING ★

Boston has a local company called Isis Parenting, and we absolutely love what it's doing on a much smaller scale. Isis, which has four locations in and around Boston, has figured out how to capture its clientele through database marketing and become the resource for everything a parent might need short of the pediatrician. It starts early: your relationship with Isis starts the moment you find out you're expecting a child. You sign up for its e-mail list and *include your due date*. That date defines you in the Isis database. With this single move, the company begins to tailor its marketing to you without needing to consider your income level.

You'll begin receiving weekly e-mails about what the baby looks like at each stage of pregnancy and, of course, tips on what sorts of products you may be interested in as you get closer to the baby's arrival. However, Isis sells not only products but also services. The services that Isis sells are like the club seats at the stadium—they're at a premium because they are wonderful. It offers everything from prenatal yoga and mommy/baby yoga to Cooking for Baby, teaching baby to sleep, nursing—you name it. If you might need it during pregnancy and after childbirth, Isis knows about it and is ready to tell you about it before you even realize it yourself.

Remember, the Club Seats Tier wants information and access; its members want to be told and sold. Isis tells its customers ahead of time, "You'll want to sign up for Cooking for Baby within the month" and "Baby Sonia would really enjoy colorful blocks at this stage to encourage her creativity and motor skills."

Its membership club allows the company to track your spending and create marketing specifically for you; each of these elements is a carefully considered revenue-generating extension. By offering 10 percent off on products and classes, Isis is more easily able to track what products and services appeal most to you, while giving you a sense of exclusivity: you may be offered preferred access to events or the ability to sign up before the general public.

Every step of the way, Isis fosters a sense of relationship and familiarity that it reinforces on a weekly basis: Isis is the only place you need to go for reliable, trustworthy parenting advice.

FINAL THOUGHTS

Remember, designating tiers and growing your database is not just about knowing who your consumer is, how much she spends, and what she likes and dislikes. No, no, no. That's how good marketers look at it. If you want to be an *exceptional* marketer and maximize the potential of your business, you have to be thinking about making customers fans of your company. This is much more intricate than having them buy your product. If you think this way and are successful with the mechanisms you created, your consumer will prefer to buy your products and services rather than your competitors'.

Ultimately, this is what every business should be thinking about all the time: (1) How do we identify and grow our customer base? (2) How do we turn those customers into fans? (3) How do we get our fans to spend more money?

Once Step 1 is complete, you then need to begin expanding your relationships with consumers and clients. Building a remarkable relationship will turn them into fans, so you will consistently be winning customers. In the next section, we will lay out what it takes to be an exceptional relationship architect.

For more ideas and resources to help you develop revenue-generating extensions for your own small company, please visit our Web site at www.louimbriano.com.

RELATIONSHIP ARCHITECTURE

BUILDING REMARKABLE BUSINESS RELATIONSHIPS

As social media marketing makes waves in business and industry, conversations about building relationships with customers and other businesses have never been more popular—or more misdirected. The ripples among customers that social media can create could have very positive or very negative effects on your business and your brand if you fail to properly approach building relationships. It doesn't matter if you have 400 Facebook friends or 4,000, or if you have 10,000 followers on Twitter. The quantity is important only if you're engaging your audience correctly, which goes well beyond frequency and friendliness.

The constant use of the words *friends*, *followers*, and *connections* has suddenly blurred what it means to build meaningful business relationships that yield large-scale results. Building relationships, what I call Relationship Architecture, has a lot less to do with collecting business cards and a lot more to do with approaching people and organizations tactically in ways that will resonate with them. Not only will you learn to design relationships carefully, but you'll also learn how to accelerate the rate at which you are able to forge those relationships: not through time, but by design.

In the next three chapters, we'll show you how to connect with people in meaningful ways and give you a look at the kind of effort it takes to create significant moments that profoundly change relationships. You already know that relationship building is important for results—executives and pundits alike always stress that business is all about relationships—but what steps do you really need to take to ensure that you are forming those relationships in ways that will yield a real change in your P&L statement or enhance the kind of influence you wield? We'll show you how we managed relationships at a billion-dollar company like the Patriots and at TrinityOne, a small boutique agency I now own. We'll show you exactly the kinds of information we collect about people, how we store that information, and how we use it.

We're also going to let you in on how to utilize relationships to maximize the spending of all of your consumers. This goes beyond getting one new person to buy one new item from you; this is about finding the people who want to change the face of your bottom line. You know that real marketing requires going well beyond rewards programs for frequent customers and perpetual e-mail blasts. In Relationship Architecture, we're going to show you how real allegiance—and real revenue—is won.

DELIVERS

When I was in radio, one of my bosses mentioned "corner store marketing," and I totally got the concept—because I had actually, quite literally, lived it. While the concept of corner store marketing may not be anything original, I have been telling this story to staff members and students for 15 years because it has led me to a deep understanding of the importance of building relationships, and now I'd like to share it with you.

I grew up in East Boston, Massachusetts, in a predominantly Italian neighborhood. We lived in a three-decker, dumbbell tenement in which my mother and my sister had to walk through my bedroom to get to their own rooms. My sister's bedroom was basically a storage room or oversized closet. There were no doors to the rooms, so there wasn't a whole lot of privacy. We lived on the third floor, and my grandparents lived on the first.

At the end of my street was this little corner store. The guy who owned and ran it was a short, potbellied, bald Italian guy named Marty. This was in the 1970s, before White Hen Pantries and Super Stop & Shops came into existence, so Marty was our butcher, our grocer, and our vegetable vendor, too.

Now, Marty didn't go to Harvard Business School or have a college degree. In fact, I would be surprised if he had a seventh-grade education; in our area, that was just a fact of life for Marty's generation. My own grandmother had to quit school after sixth grade to go to work as a seamstress to help support the family.

But that didn't mean my grandmother and Marty were not bright and intelligent. On the contrary, Marty was a pretty smart dude. His natural intelligence, coupled with his work ethic, gave him the qualities that are essential to being a successful businessperson. He seemed to live in that store; he was there whenever I stopped by. I would walk in, and Marty would jump to attention and say, "Hi, Louis, how you doin' today? Keeping your grades up in school? I saw you walk by with your sister Stephanie yesterday. You're a very good boy, the way you watch after her." He would say with a smile, "Keep studying hard, because you do not want to end up like me, sweeping up a store!"

No matter how many times I stopped by to pick up milk for my grandmother, Marty always made time to ask questions and learn more about my family. He was dedicated to us, and he showed intense interest in everything that was important to our family. He would go on, "And your grandfather, he's been a little under the weather. Is he doing OK? Anything I can do to help?"

Marty invested his time in us and in each of his other customers. He was genuinely concerned with our well-being. Maybe it was because we were his bread and butter, or maybe it was because he truly cared— which is what we believed. "How's your mother?" he would say. "I heard she wasn't doing so well. I know she was having some problems with the job, so I'm going to put a little extra in the bag. Don't worry about paying for it now. When she has a little bit more money and gets back on her feet, she can pay me then." Marty showed compassion toward us and sacrificed a bit of his own profit on our behalf. "And your sister, wasn't it her birthday the other day? She's getting so big! I remember the day she was born." He invested in his customers, and he knew more than a little about each of us—he had detailed information about our lives. Marty, a grammar school dropout, was probably one of the best customer service gurus anywhere because he understood how to build great relationships.

There was another store in our neighborhood called Frank's. Every once in a while, Frank's would have a sale or a special offer, and we would get a flyer in the mail. Frank's prices might have been a little better on some items, and we were always looking to save money. Just to give you a better feel for how tight things were money-wise: my mom used to stretch my shoes and dye them another color to get longer use out of them. It was a creative way to get new shoes. We didn't go on family vacations, and we purchased necessities, not luxuries. So, a buck here and a buck there was important. But regardless of the prices at

Frank's, even though they might have been cheaper, we would never have thought of shopping at Frank's. We shopped at Marty's no matter what. Marty was our guy, and we were loyal to him and his little store.

You might ask, "Where did Marty learn to build his business like this?" He never went to college; he never even went to high school. How did he understand that to win people over and have them respond in such a positive manner, he needed to invest in them? Truthfully, Marty didn't know any other way. He just knew that if you invested in folks, it would pay off. No gimmicks. No flair.

Marty was just honest and genuinely dedicated to his customers. It was something he just "got." It's very basic, but he intuitively understood the characteristics necessary to build a meaningful and unbreakable relationship. Marty didn't write a strategy or hold focus groups to come to these conclusions. He was just brought up to treat others well. Marty was a Relationship Architect, and he didn't even know it.

What Marty stumbled upon is a practice that, if it is executed carefully, anyone can leverage. With the right approach and the right tools, anyone can become a Relationship Architect. The basic problem is that people and organizations are not necessarily thinking about building relationships in this methodical, calculated way. This makes sense; it's easy to assume that the guy in the bodega on the corner and the company occupying offices 40 stories above him need to operate in totally different ways.

But it's not the guy in the bodega whose thinking has gone wrong.

Sure, plenty of companies talk about great customer service. Their definition of customer service is usually pretty formulaic, though: provide complete satisfaction for paying customers in the hopes that they will come back again. This kind of thinking sets the bar extremely low—so low, in fact, that companies that look beyond it are able to do just a little extra and get a lot in return. As I look around at companies in all sorts of industries, I am convinced that folks have to think about consumers, business partners, and potential customers in a deeper and more involved way. If you want customers to always be there for you, in good times and in bad, you have to become a Relationship Architect in every encounter.

You'll want to habitually think of every interaction as an opportunity to gain a new customer or build upon the relationship that you have. The capacity is in all of us; it's just that life is so busy at times that we lose sight of the endgame, growing relationships to build revenue.

I know it seems as if using Marty's skills at a major corporation might be a lot of work, but you are making a mistake if you look at becoming a Relationship Architect as a job—Relationship Architecture has to become a lifestyle.

I can hear you now: "Lou, I do everything you are saying. I already *am* a Relationship Architect."

I don't doubt that you get what I am talking about, but I doubt that the majority of folks take the concept and put it into action with the level of intensity and consistency that Marty did. Whether you're interacting with consumers or with other businesses, or you're building your network, winging it won't work.

In this chapter, we're going to talk about what it really takes to build relationships and the first steps you can take to be sure you ultimately reap everything that you possibly can from your relationship-building efforts. Since in all aspects of life, it's much easier to be successful when you have defined goals and planned mechanisms for reaching them, I've created an acronym that's designed to ensure that you're always building fruitful relationships. To this day, I can still remember the order of the planets in the solar system using the mnemonic My Very Educated Mother Just Showed Us Nine Planets (well, of course this wouldn't work now, since some rocket scientist decided to demote poor little Pluto). If a mnemonic has stuck with me for more than 30 years, I'm convinced that mnemonics work. To be a great Relationship Architect, you need to *deliver* to the relationship at every opportunity.

The great relationship builders are always thinking about how to build new and build upon relationships. But why leave the mechanism to chance? Follow the direction of my acronym DELIVERS in every encounter. Remember, all the qualities of DELIVERS work together, and, if you're careful, many of your actions will allow you to check off multiple letters toward building that unbreakable relationship.

If you're wondering, the order of the elements does not reflect any priority or pecking order. OK, let's get going.

D: DEDICATION

In order to build a remarkable business relationship, you have to be *dedicated* and genuinely give of yourself. You can't fake this; either you are present or you are not. Being dedicated is all about what is important to the person with whom you are trying to build a relationship. Dedication is all about *them*.

We have to break one of the oldest rules in the book in order to do this correctly. Most folks try to follow the advice of their grandparents, who always said, "Treat others as you would like to be treated." My apologies to my elders, but that's *wrong*! That advice is very misleading.

Don't treat others as *you* would like to be treated. Treat people the way *they* want to be treated. Your wishes and preferences have to become irrelevant if your Relationship Architecture is going to play out properly.

It's easy to find excuses for not being there. Just think of how many times you told a person, "I'll call you tomorrow," or, "See you at the game," or, "I'll stop by," and then never actually followed through on your promise. Not only is this irresponsible, but it also erodes the trust of the person you are making promises to. It's impossible for me not to think of my relationship with my kids when I talk about this level of dedication. If we tell our kids that we're going to be at a game or a school play or a function and then do not show up, they will be devastated.

Yeah, I know, "things happen" and sometimes "you just can't make it."

I'm saying, "Bullshit." If you "just can't make it," it's because you're being lazy and unprepared. "Do what you say you're going to do" needs to become the very fiber of your being. It's basically that simple.

A couple of years ago, I was in New York trying to close some business. The guy I was meeting with took a liking to me and wanted to hang out a bit longer. In other words, there was no chance that I was making my 10 p.m. flight. I had my assistant rearrange things so I got on the first flight out the next morning, around 6 a.m. Normally my staying later wouldn't be an issue, but on this particular occasion, my kids had a swim meet the next morning, and warm-ups began at 8:30 a.m. I had promised them I would be at the meet, and there was no way I wanted to disappoint them. Now, I have never missed an event of theirs that I had promised I would attend, so most people would think it was no big deal to miss just one.

However, the reality is that every time you break a promise, it erodes the relationship until finally, one day, the person you had a solid relationship with has no interest in you any longer. I have to tell you I am doing everything in my power to make sure I never break a promise.

So, this guy I'm meeting with is like the Energizer Bunny and not giving in, so I wrap up with him *extremely* late and get a car to the airport. I get on the flight, land, get my car, and proceed to drive an hour to New Hampshire, where the kids' meet was taking place. I got to the event at 9:12 a.m., in just enough time to make my son's first race. The kids were delighted. I was exhausted, but I was there, and they never knew how tired I was. I kept my promise.

If you keep all the promises you make with your kids or your best friends or your loved ones in mind and the lengths to which you will go to maintain those relationships, you will be more apt to remain dedicated to other relationships. The problem is that laziness and excuses creep into your repertoire. Don't succumb to that method of operation.

Your Individual Business Brand

What you have to understand here is a key truth about how business relationships are formed: business relationships never stop at just the individual relationships that build up your network. When you are building relationships, you are creating an image of what you represent that transcends the bonds you have with individuals. Your character and reliability must exist in the perception of everyone in your network; those perceptions define your individual business brand (IBB).

Let's focus on your IBB. The sum of all of your actions, performance, and credibility equates to your IBB. Put differently, your IBB is what others have in their heads when they think of you, the person, in tandem with the business you represent. Because of this, it is important to have a clear understanding of and vision for your individual business brand.

Some of Relationship Architecture is about tending to you, the person, and some of it is about increasing your investment in your brand. If you are not what you say you are, people will find out very quickly, and then they will rely on you, the individual, less *and* lose belief in your brand. A poor IBB kills two birds with one stone—in a bad way.

To build a solid IBB, first and foremost, without compromise, you cannot break promises. You have to create trust between you and the other person with whom you are creating a relationship, whether it's a consumer, a fan, a colleague, a superior, or a subordinate. Living up to your promises (or breaking them) will affect every aspect of you and your business. There is no neutral ground here. Your IBB has to be built on a foundation of confidence and trust.

Saying No Can Be a Positive

The primary problem in the promises business is that many people do not have the ability to say no, or "sorry, I can't." This is an enormous pitfall. Many people make commitments because they believe that a positive response is what builds a strong relationship. The fact of the matter is that "yes" has that type of outcome *only* when the result is positive as well. A negative result erodes the relationship and eventually erodes the brand. Your IBB can withstand a *few* relationship hits, but habitual missteps will absolutely crush your brand.

My pal Billy Fairweather, who used to produce *NFL Primetime* for ESPN, always riffs on the famous quote from the James Bond character Goldfinger, saying, "Once is a mistake, twice is a concern, but three times is a trend." He may have borrowed that from his old boss, Chris Berman; I'll credit them both for that spot-on observation. Because we want to avoid breaking promises at all costs, here are three simple guidelines to observe when making promises:

1. You should say yes and promise to deliver on something if and *only if* you are *certain* you can keep the promise.
2. This is key: if it's a "maybe," then you should say that you "doubt" it can be done. Use the word *doubt*. *Maybe* is much too much encouragement in the business of promises. You are much better

positioned with *doubtful*. Then, if you can make it happen, you become the hero.

3.   If your gut tells you that you cannot deliver, then say, "Sorry, I wish I could, but it's not possible," or simply, "No." If you don't respond honestly and in this manner, you are sure to be a goat, and the resulting disappointment will quickly erode your brand.

These three tips will be helpful in both guiding you to a solid foundation for your brand and keeping you dedicated to the relationships you create. The consistency of the promises you keep is essential to becoming a Relationship Architect. This dedication is crucial to your credibility and will allow you to be worthy of the relationship's trust.

Now, just knowing how and when to make promises doesn't eliminate any further responsibility to the relationship. If you are constantly saying no, you're quietly indicating the absence of any relationship at all. If you are genuinely dedicated to the relationship, whether action is requested or not, that will guarantee dedication back to you.

Dedication is only the beginning of delivering to your relationship.

E: ENERGY

Energy is an element of building relationships that I think is mistakenly taken less seriously than other characteristics of building relationships. The energy you bring to a relationship is a clear, easily controllable way to separate yourself from others. Your energy level should emanate to such a degree that the people you are engaging with know that you mean business. I'm not saying that you have to have over-the-top charisma to be a Relationship Architect (although it definitely helps), but you do have to be an upbeat presence in every encounter.

Let's face it: no one wants to be dealing with a stiff—even stiffs themselves! Not showing passion for what you believe is a huge turn-off to people; frankly, if you're not passionate about your ideas, why would anyone else be? In the same vein, people can sniff out inauthentic enthusiasm from a mile away. A good friend and general counsel for TrinityOne, Joe Vrabel, will classify folks at times as "All show and no substance." Whether you're a dead fish or the Tasmanian devil, if your energy exudes boredom or, worse, insincerity, you are not going to be capturing the hearts and minds of anyone.

Positive Energy Evokes a Positive Response

Positive energy produces positive responses. Think about all the different types of people you have met and conversed with over time. It's very hard not to like certain people. This is also probably why you have more fun with certain people when they have a few drinks in them. Let's be real: certain people who may not normally be very personable can be charming after a cocktail. Of *course* I'm not saying you should go out and get plastered before your next meeting, but let's use the knowledge that it's a lot easier to speak to people once you loosen up a bit. In the absence of alcohol, what is it that will inspire you to have positive energy when you are interacting with folks you don't know? What, as Arnold would say, "Pumps you up"?

Find Your Trigger

I'll tell you what gets me energized. Prior to meetings, I will pick a song that gets me all jacked up and blare it while I am getting ready for or driving to the meeting. Your song could be anything from "Dead or Alive" by Bon Jovi to Simon and Garfunkel's "The 59th Street Bridge Song (Feeling Groovy)." No matter what, if I pick a tune that sets the right tone, it carries me through the conversation. When you are building relationships, energy sets the tone and, most important, helps expedite the bond.

Have you ever just "hit it off" with someone? I guarantee you, there was an energy that was palpable. Think about that time for a moment. I am positive that the picture you have in your head is not of two people sitting around saying, "What do you want to do?" "I don't know; what do you want to do?"

Every individual gets "up" for a situation at one time or another. Sometimes it's just a natural high; other times you need mechanisms to help get you in the right frame of mind. Football players are experts at this; their careers ride on it. I have been on the sideline just before a game has begun, and players will be pounding each other on the shoulder pads to get the adrenaline going and the blood pumping before they take the field. It's a pretty common ritual among players. I remember vividly Tom Brady getting all over Drew Bledsoe and excitedly pushing him and pounding on his shoulder pads to get into the zone for the kick-off of Super Bowl XXXVI.

For you, pounding on someone's shoulders at work may get you fired, so I'm not recommending that; however, you have to know what it is that gets you in the right frame of mind prior to any business interaction. Find your personal trigger, that energizing song or ritual that gets you in the zone and prepared for interaction. For me, it's music. What is it for you?

L: LOYALTY

I want to take the definition of *loyalty* beyond the corniness that you're expecting. I'm not going to write about cheating or about doing business with the same people and staying true to them. Frankly, I think there's way too little of that going on these days, but you already know that. The accepted lack of loyalty is saddening; the expression, "He would sell his mother out for a buck," is more the reality.

Nevertheless, I'm convinced that *loyalty* is one of the most mis-used words in this day and age. In building relationships—unbreakable ones—loyalty is key. You have to understand this: people who are legitimately loyal are those people who spring into action on your behalf *when problems arise.*

In keeping with promoting this kind of thinking at TrinityOne, the members of my current staff aren't allowed to complain; they can only provide solutions to problems. Well, I guess they can complain, but that's when I stop listening. However, when they come to me with great ideas and solutions, then I'm all ears.

The Independent Problem Solver

The absolute best executors of this kind of loyalty don't stop at creating the solution; they implement it independently. In any relationship, there's a perfect opportunity to rise to the occasion and come to the rescue when the *you-know-what* hits the fan. In Relationship Architecture, there are many characteristics that epitomize what it takes to build a remarkable relationship, but bringing solutions to a situation forges great relationships. Action and assistance at crucial, painful moments not only are imperative for each of us to achieve success but exemplify the attitude of the Relationship Architect.

My buddy Lenny is an unbelievable Relationship Architect. He's a true "roll up his sleeves and help you solve a problem" kind of guy. He's not a big business tycoon; he has had no formal training on how to develop new relationships and maintain old ones. He just gets it. When someone needs help, he is there to provide assistance. You will find that I mention creating "memorable moments" quite often; showing loyalty when the chips are down is a no-cost, no-frills way of creating a memorable moment and becoming ingrained in the minds of others.

In the northeast Mother's Day flood of 2006, Lenny displayed the kind of loyalty that we've been talking about. The water level was at the highest it has been in 100 years at the lake—the lake that happens to be outside the back door of my family's home. The water levels were so bad that the floodwaters entered our house and water was over the beds. It was a disaster, but before anyone could think, Lenny had everything out of the house. He had one crew ripping out the walls and another crew drying, dehumidifying, and cleaning. The drying crew literally baked the house and removed all the moisture. Lenny took the bull by the horns, and before we knew it, the house was fixed up and, frankly, better than it had been before.

Lenny is not a contractor. He had no financial stake in working this out for us. Ultimately, Lenny didn't want anything in return. He was just a friend providing solutions and helping a bud out.

Lenny is The Man.

If you want to build great relationships—without any agenda or ulterior motives—be like Lenny. Everyone needs a Lenny, and if you act like he did, you will be a hero in someone's life.

I've got news for you: heroism is not something that is soon forgotten. I can never say no to Lenny because of his unselfish commitment to me. Lenny, thank you. You are a true independent solution finder and, because of that, a consummate Relationship Architect.

Do you have it in you to be a Lenny? To be loyal, all you have to do is be there no matter what is being thrown at the relationship and make it your job to find solutions to help the other person in the relationship. Forget about all the cliché crap that people think defines being loyal. Always being there to provide solutions is the essence of loyalty. Sometimes providing the solution is just being someone who will listen, who can listen to new ideas. Sometimes it means taking a more active role. No matter what it is, be there and be a Lenny.

I: INVEST

It's easy to get invested in relationships when the payoff seems obvious: if you're a new food blogger and you happen to meet an executive vice president of the Food Network, you don't need me to tell you that's a relationship you should invest in. The potential payoff from investing "up" and growing that relationship is obvious.

It's pretty typical to think that the more status a person has, the more potential there is for a rewarding relationship. You have to be in touch with reality, though: the truth is that just because a person has more stature and *could* do more for you than another doesn't mean she *will* do more.

So, instead, we're going to talk about investing *down*. The fact of the matter is, you never know which relationship is going to be "the one" that will improve your existence, and it's especially difficult to judge this at the beginning of a relationship, when we're most likely to categorize someone as useful or not. My grandfather used to always say to me, "Janitors and kings." He never said more than that, but his intention was clear: no matter what someone's status in the community is, you have to treat everyone with the same respect and genuinely invest in all types of people, no matter what their position or abilities, or how they're perceived. To be a great Relationship Architect, you cannot be proficient at building only *certain* relationships; you have to excel at building *all* relationships because you never know which ones will enrich your life.

There is no cutting corners and no magic wand for selecting the right relationships. The effort needs to be all around: janitors and kings.

I realize there are only so many hours in the day to be investing in people left and right, so in the next chapter we're going to delve into a specific system you can use to manage your personal investment in people and actionably organize your Relationship Architecture. Before we do that, though, I want to illustrate the long-term benefits of investing down. I'm going to take you back to 1987, when I had just graduated from college.

After I graduated from Boston College, I started working in radio at WHDH in Boston. I was basically a glorified gofer making $5 per hour, but I held the title of producer. Everyone was nice, but I definitely wasn't treated as someone who was at the top of the food chain. It was made abundantly clear to me that I was a rookie and had to prove myself, so I worked hard and was insatiable when it came to taking on more tasks and responsibilities. I was so enthusiastic about making the most out of my $5 an hour job that the afternoon host, Eddie Andelman, noticed me.

For those of you who are not from the Boston area or are unfamiliar with Eddie and his show, Eddie is essentially the Godfather of sports talk radio in Boston. He has a thick Boston accent and a passion for sports and food—two passions we strongly shared. Eddie took a liking to me and my "can do" attitude; I didn't understand the word *no*. Every time he asked anything of me, I jumped into Do mode.

Then, as luck would have it, Eddie's executive producer of 15 years, Bruce Cornblatt, was offered a job with Bob Costas. Eddie approached the station management and requested that I replace Bruce in the executive producer role. I was three months into the business at the time; naturally, the program director was hesitant, but he eventually caved in to the request. I became Eddie's right-hand man: he began taking me to every meeting he attended and introducing me to all the power brokers in Boston. Every day we met with a new CEO. I sat in the meetings like a sponge, listening to everything that was said, watching facial expressions, and taking in the nuances of the discussion. After the meetings (and usually on the way to grab something to eat), Eddie highlighted things that had been said, why they had been said, and how to decode the subtext of the conversation.

I was the executive producer of Eddie's show for almost 10 years. We did events together—TV shows and live broadcasts from all over the country (even one in Germany)—and we produced shows from just about every major sporting event in the United States. I didn't realize it at the time, but the experience I received and the situations he let me witness were better than any master's degree or PhD. I was a 22-year-old kid with essentially nothing but drive, and Eddie generously allowed me to network with the likes of folks that no young kid from East Boston could ever meet on his own. Eddie's unselfish attitude and willingness to invest in me as a person were major contributors to my ability to develop the business skills I possess today. I didn't make a ton of money back then, but I could never have afforded the education I received from Eddie Andelman.

One of the power brokers I met early on was Jack Connors, the CEO of Hill Holiday, one of the largest advertising firms in the country. I remember eating lunch in his office in the John Hancock Tower overlooking the Charles River and the city of Boston, and getting the feeling from both Jack and Eddie that I was welcome and that I belonged. I'll tell you, that went a long way toward boosting the business confidence of a kid just out of college. Here's the incredible part: from that day on, whenever I bumped into Jack Connors, he always remembered who I was—by name—and was unbelievably gracious to me. After I started working with the Patriots, I saw Mr. Connors at the Four Seasons in Boston; he stopped, said hello, and then proceeded to tell me that he had been following my career. He said that he was thrilled about my success and to keep up the great work. Amazing.

What's even more amazing is that there is a list of other wildly successful people Eddie introduced me to who have treated me similarly. Each meeting Eddie took me to built my equity with the leaders he was meeting with. Beyond that, it instilled in me the confidence to be able to take a meeting with anyone, regardless of title or wealth. These guys invested their time, experience, and connections in me, and because of that, there's nothing I wouldn't do for them.

Eventually, as all things do, Eddie's investment in me came full circle. In the course of all the radio shows and events we produced, Eddie and I formed a TV production company through which we created and owned a number of TV shows in the Boston area. In fact, one of the shows, *Phantom Gourmet*, is still on the air and very successful. Once I made the move to the Patriots, Eddie asked to meet with me, and in that meeting, he asked me to sell my interest in the production company.

To be completely honest, I really didn't want to sell, because I had worked very hard to create, format, produce, and market the shows, and I wanted to continue to be involved—and, quite frankly, to reap the financial and professional benefits. But at one point in the conversation, Eddie looked at me and said, "It would be a big favor to me, because I would like to set up the boys [his three sons], give it to them, and have them work together."

Enough said. As much as it pained me to let go from both an ownership and a financial perspective, I couldn't say no after all that Eddie had done for me. I realized that the opportunity and education he had provided me with were much more valuable than a few TV shows. Some may say that I got the short end of the deal with that transaction, but they didn't experience the selfless giving that Eddie had bestowed upon me throughout the years we worked together. My selling my share in the company was still not enough repayment, as far as I'm concerned. And even though we haven't worked together in more than 15 years, I know that if I ever needed him, he would be there for me, and I for him.

Investment is the mechanism for breeding loyalty. If you give, you will get 10 times as much in return. To possess unbreakable relationships that lead to success, invest in people and genuinely give of yourself. Simple.

V: VISION

As we talked about in the section on investing in people, people get caught up in trying to figure out at the handshake who will be the "right" person to network with and who will be able to help them the most. The fact of the matter is, you just never know. I have had big executives full of talk and promises do nothing for me and doormen open the doors to great opportunities. Everyone matters, so you have to treat every relationship as if it will be the one to make a difference. The skill that Eddie possessed—and that every great Relationship Architect cultivates—is the *vision* to see beyond the status of an individual or his title. A person's present status is irrelevant in the relationship-building business.

When I was growing up, my dad had a close friend and neighbor, Arthur Tacelli, who was an attorney in Boston. Mr. Tacelli, as I called him, was a great guy who always had great stories. He was a "street" guy, but he was very intelligent, and he loved to discuss matters of principle. For some reason, Arthur took a liking to me and loved to chat me up. He would question me as if I were one of his witnesses ("So why do you think that, sir?" or, "What is the reasoning behind this?"), and we would spend time exploring different concepts and ideas.

Among all the stories, there's one that has just stuck with me since college. Arthur has a daughter, Carla, who is around my age. Carla traveled into Boston each day to get to school. Anyone who is familiar with East Boston knows that the area is basically an island, so to get downtown, one must go through the Sumner Tunnel. Prior to the Big Dig, this was a nightmare (I know firsthand because I went through it every day to get to BC). Traffic was typically backed up like crazy, and proceeding through the tunnel was slow, to say the least. Quite often, Carla found herself stopped at the tollbooth, and being a very nice and pleasant young lady, she would try to strike up a conversation.

There was this one toll taker she saw essentially every morning. This dude lived a cranky, miserable existence, and he always had a frown on his face. Carla, not being the least bit judgmental, was as friendly to him as she was to anyone, and each morning she greeted "the Crank" with a cheerful, "Good morning!" Day after day she got nothing in return: no smile, no nod, nothing. Now, I never witnessed any of this, but I know Carla, and I can just envision her being as pleasant and nice as can be. This guy had to be ultramiserable to not say hello back.

Carla told her father, Arthur, about the toll taker and about how she had decided to make it her mission to get him to say hello. Day in and day out she would greet the Crank in some new way in an effort to provoke him to say hello. One day, Carla noticed a Dunkin' Donuts cup in the booth, and it gave her an idea. The next day, along with her bright and shiny, "Good morning," she handed the toll taker a cup of coffee along with the toll. The coffee was black, and alongside it were cream and sweetener so he could have it just the way he wanted it. The Crank was stymied as Carla drove off in satisfaction, hoping the next day would produce different results.

Sure enough, the next day at the tollbooth, Carla was greeted with a big smile and "Good morning," along with a thank you. From then on, the miserable toll taker was pleasant and friendly to Carla as she drove by. Carla had set her goal for this particular relationship and had stuck to the vision. She hadn't let anything sway her, and she was relentless in her pursuit of it.

Arthur was thrilled and proud to tell me that story, and, in typical Mr. Tacelli fashion, he questioned me on the lesson learned. We bantered back and forth, and he finished off by punctuating the lesson. "Louis, always remember—never, ever give in, and never, ever let anyone change your positive behavior, what you believe in, and your vision to see it through."

I would love to tell you that this toll taker became a billionaire and hired Carla to run his businesses, but that's just not real. Still, the story taught me to approach every relationship with a plan that captures where you want it to be and to see that plan through to the end. You are not going to hit it big with every relationship you build. In fact, many relationships will not end up the way you planned, but the point is that you should never change how you approach each and every relationship you enter into.

Vision is not about reward; it's about seeing the value of building every relationship so that the relationship itself is completely solid. This is about another link in your chain of relationships. Many people lose sight of this notion and revert back to the specific payday. True vision will get you past that and focused on what truly matters.

E: ENGAGE AND ENTERTAIN

OK, so I threw a bonus "E" into the mix. I am a big believer in the idea that you have to *entertain*, even if it's just for a moment, to fully *engage* the person you are building a relationship with. If you do a simple thing like making someone smile, he will feel more connected to you. Let's repeat that: the entire purpose of engaging with others is to get them to feel connected to you. Being a little bit entertaining has to become habitual, a part of your lifestyle. The key is for people to remember you in a positive light, as someone they enjoyed being around before and would like to be around *again*.

Social media are a great way to practice relationship engagement. The principles of solid social media engagement mesh perfectly with a carefully constructed Relationship Architecture.

Admittedly, I was dragged into the world of social media kicking and screaming. I was resistant because I viewed it as an incredible time suck (which, by the way, it is). But I am truly glad Kelly Downing convinced me to participate, because even though I was right about the time commitment, everything worthwhile calls for the investment of time. It's just how you use that time that ensures it is worthwhile.

If you know me even a little, you know that when I do something, I always put 200 percent of myself into it, which I believe is a major factor in social media turning out to be such a positive experience. I can't vouch for their effectiveness if you're not going to throw yourself into them. That being said, the world of social media in and of itself has made a visibly positive difference in my life. Most important, it has reinforced the idea that engagement keeps you on people's radar, which invariably leads to potential business.

You know that old saying, out of sight, out of mind? Man, that is incredibly true. If you are not engaging, you are missing opportunities.

EXTRA POINTS

I wrote an e-book discussing the five Ps of sports and social media. My purpose was to create helpful guidelines to assist those at teams in navigating through the world of social media, but the reality is that the five Ps are great reminders to assist you in engaging with any business relationship. The e-book is free, and you can access it here: http://louimbriano.com/winningthecustomer-reference.

We're going to devote all of Chapter 6 to delving into what I believe is the most effective way to engage with people and remain on their radar: creating memorable moments. Memorable moments are strategically developed experiences with people that ensure that you stay in their minds *forever*—they're all about creating an indelible impression.

R: RESPONSIBILITY

The "R" in DELIVERS is a tough one: you are going to have to be the one to take the *responsibility* for the relationship. Remember, building remarkable business relationships is a business practice of forging unbreakable relationships *by design* as opposed to *over time*. Design and tactical relationship building require the sense of responsibility to look beyond the pettiness and scorekeeping mindsets of, "Well, I called the last three times, and now it's her turn to call me," or, "I invited him to three games, and he hasn't invited me anywhere." Forging a business relationship is not about you.

Let me say that again, because it's important: *it's not about you; it's about the relationship.*

It's easy to fall into the trap of thinking the way you might in your everyday relationship building on this one, because those relationships are predicated on give and take. Tactical Relationship Architecture is different: you cannot view Relationship Architecture as standard operating procedure. The goal is to be building relationships constantly, even if you're the one doing all the work, because the sum total of all your relationships will bring the ultimate reward. When I was with the New England Patriots, we owned the rights to the preseason games, which meant we produced the games and placed them on a local TV station. Typically, we controlled three of the four games, with one being picked up by the network. One year, while prepping for the first game, I phoned one of the men who produced the TV features that highlighted our sponsors during the broadcast. The purpose of the call was to gauge their progress and to see if everything was ready for game one.

Well, they were lagging behind a bit and I was concerned about their efforts, so I let that be known. My contact understood my concerns and promised that everything would be completed and looking great for game time. Then, not to be one-upped, he shot one across my bow, mentioning that he noticed that the "log looked a little light," which meant that we hadn't sold all of the commercial spots for the game. If you are unfamiliar with the term, "the log" is a printout that documents all of the available advertising slots during a broadcast. My group was responsible for selling spots and features for the broadcast.

I told him not to worry about how many spots were sold and to just complete the features to be produced, but he decided to push me. "You know, spots are like an unsold airline ticket. Once the plane takes off, you lose that money." This is traditionally how many broadcasters have viewed inventory, but it is not how Relationship Architects view it. Now, in all fairness to my colleague, sales of television commercials is quite different from revenue generation for an NFL team—at least, when an NFL team is doing it the way it should. I felt it was time to shed a little light on this Dark Ages view of revenue generation.

I let loose. I told him that we sold spots, features, signs, and logo rights to realize revenue, but we approached it as Relationship Architects and never force-fed inventory just because we had a glut of it. We created programs to fit with our partners' needs and help them achieve their goals.

Here comes the funny part—he said to me, "You lose that opportunity for revenue once a spot goes unsold when the game airs. DO YOU GET IT?" I still laugh thinking about it. You've got to like the chutzpah of this guy. But now it was time to school him.

So I said, "Oh, I *get it*, and I also *get* that *that* rationale is exactly how most teams and leagues fail. They sell their inventory without thought or consideration of the sponsors' needs, regardless of the outcome. That's the old way of doing business, and anyone who is doing it that way will soon be looking for a new job. I really don't care what inventory we sell and whom we sell it to. What I am concerned with is that we are *adding* more partners each year and *keeping* the partners we have.

"To do that, and to do it right, we need to think about what will best help our partners do business. If we do that, then we will grow our revenues. We are showing a 25 percent growth in revenue over last year, we added 12 new partners this spring, and we'll probably be at even higher numbers by the time the regular season begins. Meanwhile, *you* are scrambling to produce the features of the partners who pay your salary. So, the question is, do YOU get it?"

The perfect ending of the story is that, although he was completely nonplussed at the time, my colleague soon came to understand the importance of serving our partners and see it like an automated task. His group began to work more closely with ours to ensure that our partners received what was best for them. At the end of the day, that's what's best for the team.

The inventory you sell, whether it's anvils or airtime, should not be the focus of your efforts. What you get out of each individual relationship is not what matters, either.

Building relationships is central to your growth. Relationships equal revenue, so it's your responsibility not to force-feed your potential clients to purchase what *you* want to sell them. You have to provide them with what *they* need. If you force what you are trying to sell down people's throats, they're only going to spit it back at you. We're going to look further at how to sell to budgets instead of inventory in the next section, because it's important to keep in mind that although we are building these relationships to build revenue, you can't focus solely on the revenue or the vehicles you utilize to recognize revenue.

Relationship Architects don't sell. They build.

Great Relationship Architects deliver, but an exceptional Relationship Architect DELIVERS. Martin Luther King, Jr., said, *"The ultimate measure of a man is not where he stands in moments of comfort and convenience, but where he stands at times of challenge and controversy."* These words ring true in any form of relationship building, but they absolutely define the remarkable Relationship Architect. Let's look at the last piece now.

S: SACRIFICE

The "S" in DELIVERS, *sacrifice*, is the wild card that will separate you from the pack in any relationship. When you sacrifice yourself for another, you're waving the magic wand of relationship building. Think about anyone who has gone to bat for you and helped you with total disregard for her own interests and agenda. Think of how you feel about that person. *That* is powerful. When you sacrifice for another person, it makes it almost impossible for her to forget you and not do everything in her power to help you in any way that she can. Where you "stand at times of challenge and controversy" defines who you are as a person and what you will ultimately mean to other people.

When I was running Marketing for the Patriots, one of my guys got into a little jam. Well, let's just say that over the years, a bunch of my guys got into jams, but that was part of the way we did business. We worked hard and played hard; it was the atmosphere we created specifically to breed a team atmosphere that allowed us to accomplish more than anyone expected.

Well, this guy, let's call him Xavier, did something that upset the owners. He made a bad judgment call—a *significantly* bad judgment call.

The situation was obviously a bit more complicated than I'm letting on, but this isn't a "tell all the dirt" book, and giving you the details would turn this thing into the *National Enquirer.* So trust me, without all the details, in a normal situation, Xavier would have been out the door. The owners weren't too pleased with his actions, and rightfully so. They wanted to fire Xavier.

The problem was that Xavier was working with me and had been incredibly loyal to me for a few years. He was a go-to guy in a lot of the same ways I had been for Eddie Andelman; anytime I asked him for something, he always came through. Now, the owners never experienced that on a day-to-day basis, so it's easy to see why they would judge Xavier on one specific, particularly bad incident. Again, I am not questioning their rationale or their reasoning; I understood it, and I am not saying that they were wrong. They pressed the issue of firing Xavier with me harder than they had pressed any issue about anyone who worked for me.

I expressed to the owners that not firing him meant so much to me that if they insisted that I do so, while I understood their motivation, I would have to leave as well. I put my neck on the line for Xavier—and the fact that I knew all along that this story could have ended differently is what defined my actions as being authentically sacrificial.

Saying that I'd have to leave the company too wasn't a threat; that never would have flown. I was sincere, and I stated my case thoughtfully. To the credit of ownership, they told me that although they had specific thoughts about the course of action that should be taken, they trusted my judgment and that I would handle it appropriately.

Xavier caught my displeasure, but he was allowed to keep his job, and he made incredible contributions to the organization thereafter—contributions that far outweighed his mistakes. Xavier knows I went to bat for him (although I'm not sure if he knows to what extent), but there is no doubt that my sacrifice will stay with him forever and that, any time I asked, he would be there for me.

Sacrifice, like most aspects of DELIVERS, is all about paying attention and taking action when the relationship needs tending, no matter what the cost.

RELATIONSHIP ARCHITECTURE IS A DISCIPLINE

Relationship Architecture is not brain surgery, and it's certainly not some long-lost ancient Chinese secret we've unearthed. Relationship Architecture is a *discipline*, and DELIVERS is a method of organizing the practice of that discipline to ensure that you pay attention to and nurture your relationships in a manner that will allow you to grow your network and flourish in business.

Successful Relationship Architects get past the laziness, forget about how others operate, and focus on delivering to their business relationships on a daily basis. Most people are so focused on the *purpose* of growing their business that they lose sight of the *person*. It's time to reset the pins. Use DELIVERS to strike to the core of building remarkable business relationships.

THE TEN COMMANDMENTS OF RELATIONSHIP BUILDING

Just as successfully building one's dream home requires an architect to create a detailed blueprint, envisioning a relationship in its final form is crucial for building that relationship successfully. To ensure that the built home reflects his design and is as appropriate as possible for the family who will live in it, an architect chooses every element and requires that every dimension and choice be drawn to exacting standards. All the materials necessary to achieve the final goal are thought through and determined well before the building process commences. Once that vision has been captured in a blueprint, then and only then can construction begin.

The same is true with a strategic business relationship. It's key to understand that even though the perception is that most unbreakable relationships take many years to form, these relationships can also be developed in a relatively brief time *by design*. Speeding up a natural process is incredibly valuable—and achievable—if you approach it with the forethought and planning of an architect, a Relationship Architect. The path to success begins with envisioning the relationship and planning its progress and its ultimate destination. Forming an unbreakable relationship in an abbreviated period of time is very achievable.

THE ART OF THE ICEBREAKER

If you've never seen a Super Bowl ring up close, they're enormous and *extremely* gaudy. I wear one of my rings every day, partly because it's fun and partly because it's a great conversation piece: when people see it, they invariably ask about it, want to hold it, and love to try it on. My Super Bowl ring is a great icebreaker that gives me an advantage in engaging people in conversation about a topic that's exciting *and* related to my business. For me, wearing a Super Bowl ring is a game changer.

Of course, not everyone has the luxury of having such a high-impact tool that easily prompts engagement, but that doesn't mean that not having a Super Bowl ring puts you at a disadvantage. Before I had the ring, I simply had to be a bit more creative in breaking the ice to start a conversation.

When I worked in radio, my job was to book guests for a sports station in Boston, Sports Radio 850 WEEI, and every year we aired remote broadcasts from the Super Bowl. Because so many celebrities and athletes attend the Super Bowl, the event was target-rich, and prospects for having great guests on the show were high. In fact, when we first started broadcasting on location at the Super Bowl, it was very easy to book guests. There were only three to five stations broadcasting from the lobby of NFL headquarters, so as celebrities walked by, they'd stop and spend 10 or 15 minutes at each station. Over the years, more and more stations caught on, and things became much more competitive. It got to the point where dozens of stations were lined up in an area called "Radio Row"; in fact, it got so intense that the high-profile talent would pointedly avoid the lobby in fear of being trapped for hours with radio crews.

Naturally, if celebs were promoting an initiative, a book, or a product, they'd be more likely to make the rounds at Radio Row, but the overall trend was for major athletes and celebrities to avoid the area. One year, former Raider and current Fox broadcaster Howie Long must have lost his way and ended up in the lobby before the game. The buzzards smelled fresh meat and began to circle. Howie walked past the stations as swiftly as possible, to the sounds of desperate radio producers yelling, "Mr. Long, Mr. Long! Hey, Howie! Please join us on WXXX or KNNN." Head down, Howie made a beeline for the elevators to escape being picked clean.

Fortunately, I was a veteran of the Radio Row game—albeit just as much of a circling killer—and I had spent some time prepping and developing icebreakers to catch the attention of my targets. During brief encounters, you have only so much time to snag and capture, so you have to be concise but poignant. I swooped in next to the former gridiron giant and Massachusetts native, jumping into the elevator with him. As soon as the doors closed, I said, "We have mutual friends." He looked at me, obviously tired of being harassed, and said, "I doubt that could be possible."

I know it sounds like Howie was being rude, but you have to understand that at this point, he had had 50 radio producers clawing at him, and I absolutely empathized with the guy.

But I still had a job to do.

Very calmly and casually, I said, "Well, I guess I will tell Herb Wenzel that you don't remember him."

It was as though the elevator had come to a complete stop. With that one name mentioned, this huge, aggravated quarterback-sacking machine turned to me with a warm smile on his face and exclaimed, "Herb Wenzel?! How the hell is he? Herb is a great guy." I explained how I knew Herb and what he was up to. Then, just when the moment was perfect, I made my dive: I asked Howie if he could join us on Sports Radio WEEI from Boston, his hometown station. He was so caught up in reminiscing about the old days and great memories that he couldn't say no.

It might make you chuckle to hear that, as a teenager, Howie's dad had worked for Herb Wenzel as a lifeguard at the beach where I was a lifeguard years later. Herb's son, Michael, was the best man at my wedding, and he had coincidentally mentioned their connection to me just prior to my trip to the Super Bowl. Preparation is important, but luck is better than skill any day.

Sometimes you make your own luck.

Just like that, Howie Long came back downstairs and joined us on the air. He was fun and entertaining—it was an awesome interview. As he stood to say good-bye, I shot a look at the other buzzards around the lobby, warning them to back off from my kill, and they obliged as a sign of respect for my successful hunt. Howie jumped into the elevator, not to be seen again until the pregame show aired on Fox.

I didn't have a Super Bowl ring in those days, but I consistently created icebreakers through hard work and solid background research. Sure, the encounter with Howie leaned toward luck, but it definitely made me realize that with a little effort, anyone can pull out a nugget of information that cracks the hard shell of his next Howie Long.

This kind of background research became a regular practice for me and was the foundation of my philosophy when I joined the New England Patriots. In radio, I'd had to convince someone to give me five or ten minutes of his time and I had only a moment to be really compelling. I had to be incredibly good at thinking fast and knowing my stuff, because at the end of the day, it was my job to convince guests to be on the air. Learning these skills in a smaller, fast-paced framework—a quick fact or comment would get me 15 minutes of someone's time—equipped me to enter the world of the NFL with a fresh perspective. We realized that the deeper we took our research to find potential icebreakers and background information about a customer or a potential client, the higher the walls we were able to break down; the approach changed how business was done at the team, transforming it into a model that was purely relationship-oriented—and very profitable.

Over the course of a decade, we refined the model scientifically, pointedly collecting information and refining this targeted approach to all of our business relationships.

It Takes Only One Change in a Process to Make a Difference

When I was a freshman at Boston College High School, I struggled to keep my grades up. What little process I had developed to get myself from taking notes in class to retaining real knowledge just wasn't working. I was totally unprepared for the rigors of BC High. One day I missed a class and had to copy notes from a bud; as I reviewed his notes, my own problem became clear to me. His handwriting was atrocious, and it took me what felt like ages to read his notes carefully and rewrite them in my notebook. However, as I wrote, I noticed that the section that I copied slowly in my own notebook was much more legible—far more so than the notes I had jotted down during other classes. Even as I was writing, I could tell that the material was beginning to stick.

I began to think differently and changed the way I was taking notes in class. I added a new notebook to the mix, taking very fast notes that were a bit sloppy and shorthand in class, then rewriting them in a different notebook in a much more deliberate and organized fashion later that night. The transfer from one notebook to the other helped amazingly with my retention of knowledge on my subjects. It makes absolute sense—the constant repetition was helping me remember—but it was remarkable how much difference that one little step made in improving my grades. That simple system helped me achieve my goals in high school, and building business relations is not much different: if you put simple systems in place, you can grow relationships that help you achieve your goals.

Business relationships usually fail even before they begin. Quite often, a meeting with a potential new business contact is so fleeting that virtually no thought is given to structuring the relationship, and there is no follow-through. Everyone has time constraints, and unless they foresee a clear business opportunity, most people don't give a second thought to the new relationship. This is a mistake. It may seem painfully simple, but follow-through is absolutely necessary to form a mutually beneficial, long-lasting relationship.

Relationship Architecture requires that forethought and systematic planning go into forging a remarkable business relationship. If you lay the proper groundwork, you help to ensure that the relationship will be fruitful in one way or another.

How many business cards do you have in your possession or contacts in your Outlook where you have never followed up with the people you got them from after that initial meeting? If you have met as many people as I have throughout my career, that number could be mind-boggling. I'll be the first to admit that over the years, I have squandered many initial meetings and didn't invest in each the way I should have. I reiterate: this is a big mistake.

Controlling the Process

During the early years when I was with the Patriots, I was meeting so many new people that I let myself believe there was no way I could remember everyone. I felt inundated with introductions that amounted to smiles and nods; I never even heard the person's name or whom he worked for unless the name or the title triggered dollar signs. I let the numbers control me instead of me controlling the process with preparation and follow-through. I don't say this often, and I know you'll be getting up off the ground after falling off your seat—but I was dead wrong!

Because the number of people I met was astronomical, I gave in to the notion that I could never cultivate relationships with everyone. That was just pure laziness. When I was in radio, I had been a great relationship builder. While I was performing at a higher level during these early years at the Patriots, it still didn't feel like I was "on" in my icebreaking and relationship building the way I'd been in radio. Then, one day, it hit me: I came to terms with the relationship squandering to which I had reverted and became determined to devise a system that would allow me to manage the volume and not let a single, potentially valuable relationship fall through the cracks. I knew that I had to make adjustments and remake myself.

I needed to recapture the *precision* of my earliest icebreaking efforts while expanding the *number* of relationships that I had built. I decided to retool the note-taking system that had aided me so much in high school and college and use that as a foundation for fine-tuning a system to capture and retain information for business relationships.

As I refined the system, I found folks marveling at what I remembered about them, and every time I stuck to the system, I was a far better Relationship Architect. This system has evolved over time and is now a 10-step process; the system I'm about to show you is exactly what we were using at the Patriots, and it's the same one we employ at TrinityOne to manage our relationship building.

I went to Catholic school my entire life, and my references often reflect that. With that said, I call this process the *Ten Commandments of Organizing a Business Relationship*. If you organize your life, everything proceeds more smoothly. Organizing a growing relationship is no different.

THE TEN COMMANDMENTS OF ORGANIZING A BUSINESS RELATIONSHIP

1. Thou shouldst always review the business card of anyone you meet.
2. Create a file and a system to capture information about the relationship.

3. Follow up with any person you meet.
4. Honor your relationship and gather information.
5. Thou shalt not stop here.
6. Send periodic notes to keep communication flowing.
7. Surprise people by remembering something that is very important to them.
8. Invite people to an event that you can attend together.
9. See that what you do DELIVERS to the relationship.
10. Repeat Commandments 6 through 9 on a consistent basis.

These Ten Commandments are pretty basic, extremely practical, and very achievable. The relationship business is not nuclear physics, but you need to be disciplined and adhere to this practice if you want to be a successful Relationship Architect. The commandments are designed to serve as a mechanism that helps you stay true to the mission of building unbreakable business relationships.

1. Thou Shouldst Always Review the Business Card of Anyone You Meet

I can already hear you saying, "Is this guy for real? Of course I review the business cards I receive. How is this even remotely helpful?"

I'm going to pause here and call out, "Bullshit." The reality is that you get the card, give it a quick glance, and shove it in your pocket. Then, at a later date, some intern either types it into your Outlook or tapes it into your Rolodex. Maybe, just maybe, you are the person typing it into your BlackBerry. But the question you have to ask yourself is, once you hit "save" and it's locked securely into your device of choice, what's next? The fact of the matter is that many people stop here, and if you stop, there's a very good chance that the relationship will never flourish.

A real business card review is totally different. Your first course of action, the very next day, is to take out that business card. Don't just record the information, but *jot down notes from the conversation* you had with the individual. Don't focus on the contact information and the dollar sign potential attached to it; you need to be thinking about how this contact fits into your network and your chain of relationships. That's not to say that your initial thought here is the only possible direction for the relationship, but pausing at this step enhances the potential for the new contact to become a solid business relationship in reality. Reviewing the business card is not about glancing at the information printed on the card stock; it's about taking stock of the potential of the relationship.

If you turn your nose up at this First Commandment, you are liable to squander a potential opportunity. This is a moment to embrace the "janitors and kings" philosophy we talked about in Chapter 4; you never really know where the next great relationship will sprout, so treat everyone like it's the next great meeting. That attitude changes the game for you.

I left the New England Patriots in April 2006, and in May of the same year, my wife, Patricia, and I went to the Kentucky Derby—half for business, half for pleasure. We had always been horse racing fans, but we felt that with the launching of TrinityOne, attending the Derby would be a good opportunity to connect with potential clients and see some longtime friends.

Having been with the Patriots for so many years, we had a few connections, and we got into a number of the festivities leading up to the Derby. One night we were hanging out at an event with a pal and former partner, Michael O'Hara Lynch, senior vice president of global sponsorship for Visa, when we happened to bump into a group of Patriots players. Now, while I was at the team for a decade, my job wasn't to hang around with the players; my job was to build the brand, relationships, and revenue. It wasn't like I was a friend of theirs. Sure, at times we acknowledged one another walking through the halls, but we were not going out and having coffee together. It's not how the organization was set up.

Because of this dynamic, I didn't go out of my way to strike up conversations with the players at the party; it just wouldn't have been authentic, and to be honest, I don't think they needed any additional friends. So we basically kept to ourselves.

I have to say that I was more than surprised when a few of the players acknowledged us and came over to say hello and wish us well. I honestly didn't think most of them knew who I was. The real kicker was when the quarterback made his way over. Tom Brady walked over with a big smile, shook my hand, gave Patricia a kiss, and proceeded to ask us questions about the new company and how we were. He knew things that he wouldn't have known unless he was paying attention. It was very nice of him to say hello and show a genuine interest; it wasn't as if we were long-lost friends. He certainly didn't need anything from me, and if he hadn't said hello and chatted, I would have thought nothing of it and not thought less of him for failing to do so.

At that moment, I knew that Tom Brady was a Relationship Architect. He probably didn't have any ulterior motives, but he still seized the opportunity to make an impression so that we would remember him in a positive light. During the 10 minutes he spent with us, his stock with us rose dramatically. It wasn't phony; it wasn't contrived. He just made a conscious decision to be a Relationship Architect.

It turned out that Brady had been smart to do so, because two years later, when he went down with a season-ending injury, business reporters were calling me asking how the injury affected Tom's marketability. It made sense; I was a sports marketing veteran and professor, and they wanted to know my take. I didn't hesitate to positively position Brady as the one player I would want to endorse my product and services if I were a brand manager for a big company. I believed wholeheartedly in what I was saying, but I absolutely know that my positive experience with him absolutely skewed my comments that much further in his favor.

It makes sense to me that Brady would understand the principles of being a Relationship Architect, because as a leader of a team and a game planner, he had all of the characteristics necessary to be great at building relationships. If you know how to be a game planner, you can win the relationship too.

2. Create a File and a System to Capture Information about the Relationship

After you have gathered information about the new potential relationship, creating an effective filing system is crucial to building a remarkable business relationship. When I was with the Patriots, and even in the early days of TrinityOne, I called my assistant immediately after leaving every meeting and gave him a complete rundown of all the information I had gathered, noting what I thought was important from the encounter.

I even jotted down notes during the meeting to trigger my memory on what should be included in this person's profile.

Now, with the ever-changing advances in technology, I can do all this in a much more streamlined manner. I have been using the Dragon dictation system, which allows me to record my thoughts orally and send them in an e-mail to be captured and inserted into profiles. This method is much more efficient and works quite nicely.

The key to gathering information about current and potential relationships is to develop a profile system that captures varying levels of information to help you fully understand the individual and the company that she works for. The profile's structure really illuminates how business and personal lives intersect in the relationship-building business. There is no detail that is unimportant, so make sure that you capture the characteristics of the contact, his likes and dislikes, and as many details you can dig up to build your arsenal.

The name of her college sorority is important.

His affinity for ice cream means something.

When you are kicking things off, it really doesn't matter if you're storing your data in something as basic as a handwritten notebook of names and information or taking it to the next level with FileMaker, Excel, or Outlook. You can take it even further and use a customer relationship management system such as Salesforce. Just make sure you have a system to help you gather and capture information and think about how big you may need it to get as your company grows.

When we initiated this practice with the New England Patriots, we first focused on the corporate sponsors. The information we were gathering lived in these huge binders broken down by company; within each was all the information about the company relationships and the individuals who worked there. Over the course of time, we computerized every profile so that this information was at our fingertips and connected to our database. We adopted the axiom that "information is power." As we grew, we began adding other levels of the organization's customers to our customer relationship management system.

We ultimately created the Web-based system dedicated to understanding and building relationships using ONYX that we talked about in detail in Chapter 1. Eventually, we had a five-person group whose sole purpose was to manage the system and the information input. This group could pull information on any customer and potential client in moments to fully prepare anyone who was going into a meeting. Our goal was to equip anyone in our organization to manage the relationship at any point, using the details we had archived.

Ensuring that the system could be useful to anyone who tapped into it was smart not only for the sales point person on the account, but also for the team and its relationship longevity. Many organizations lose clients when their main point of contact departs from the company. The relationship typically thrives through the efforts of an individual, but it's in the company's interest to protect the relationship so that the relationship is with the *company*, not the person. Creating a profiling system is beneficial not only for the folks who are building, maintaining, and growing the relationship, but also for the company that needs and ultimately owns the relationship.

You cannot take it for granted that a relationship will stay with your organization when the lead on that relationship departs. We built the system at the Patriots to serve both the employees and the team. It's a well-known fact that people prefer to do business with others they know and trust—the database system you put in place enables that to happen.

EXTRA POINTS
We've put together a sample TrinityOne database profile that you may like to use as a springboard for creating your own database. You can find it at http://louimbriano.com/ winningthecustomer-reference.

3. Follow Up with Any Person You Meet

Quite often when you meet a new person, if there isn't immediate gratification or the near promise of it, your follow-through is dismal. You have to break out of that bad habit and begin following up with everyone you meet on some level. When it appears that a person may not be able to contribute to your business growth, don't just end the relationship there. A business relationship is like New England weather: wait a minute and it will change. Even if there does not appear to be any synergy with the person you just met at the moment, do not discard the opportunity.

After you meet someone

1. Shoot the person a quick note.
2. Not only mention that it was nice to meet her, but also include small details of the conversation when possible.

These two simple action items will be enough to catch the person's attention, put you in a positive light, and keep you on her radar. There is no downside to taking these quick extra steps to try to forge a relationship.

At this stage of the game, you should also have a course of action for every person you meet. Think about putting each relationship at its inception into one of three buckets. Let's call them the "Don't Let the Relationship Kick the Bucket Buckets." Here's how you should differentiate the levels:

★ Bucket 1 is a relationship that needs immediate attention and action.
★ Bucket 2 is a potential relationship in the future.
★ Bucket 3 is the "you just never know" group.

Once you subdivide your new relationships into buckets, you can begin working on growing each relationship in the appropriate manner—without spending too much time on the long shots, but still giving everyone an appropriate amount of attention. Stick to a follow-up methodology that fits with each bucket and stay the course. How you do this has to be in line with who you are as an individual. You just can't force it and be someone you are not. You may use e-mail, calling, letter writing, or texting; the "how" is not important at this juncture. The key to this commandment is to always follow up, and if someone reaches out to you, always respond.

4. Honor Your Relationship and Gather Information

If you completed the Second Commandment, you now have a system for collecting and saving information about the relationship on a consistent basis. Here's where a well-thought-out system to capture information is imperative. To be an exceptional Relationship Architect, it's not good enough to merely understand the individual's business habits and practices or the superficial details of his personal life. You need to delve deeper and know aspects of his life beyond what he shares with you. Each profile you create should begin with the research that you or your team did on the individual and the company he works for. That company info should include detailed information about goals, organizational structure—any information that gives you insight into how the company operates. The individual information you get from Google searches and news articles is a fine beginning, but it's just the beginning.

Don't Give In to Incomplete Information You have to be dedicated to gathering as much pertinent information as possible; look at gathering information as an expression of your enthusiasm for growing your business. The data you gather will be the resource that enables you to build an unbelievable relationship. Every encounter should be viewed not as another meeting to try to seal a deal, but instead as an expedition from which you'll mine information concerning the person that can be used as the building blocks of your unbreakable business relationship. It's easy to cut corners and let laziness creep in at this stage, but you can't give in to incomplete information.

You also need to remember that more often than not, extracting information from people requires that you provide information and slivers of yourself as well. In fact, if you are genuine and real, the more you give, the more you get. When you are creating a business relationship, you still have to get personal.

Get Used to Getting Personal When I was a producer for Eddie Andelman, "The Dean of Sports Talk Radio," after I got out of college, my job was to call agents, athletes, celebrities, and noteworthy businesspeople to get them to come on the show and join Eddie in conversation. This was a totally different ball of wax from trying to snag people for a pre-Super Bowl interview. Getting folks to come on the radio to talk about themselves may seem like an easy task, but it was not. Most of the people I was calling I had never met before, so quite often it was the ultimate cold call. It took complete persistence, but more than that, the potential guests had to feel comfortable with me and trust that coming on Eddie's show would be a positive experience.

This was back in the late 1980s, so we did not have e-mail, Google, or Twitter to streamline connecting with folks. All we had was the trusty old fully wired phone.

The biggest problem I found was that when I made the call, I never knew who was going to pick up. Sometimes I'd get an assistant, but other times it was a spouse or even a child. No matter who picked up the phone, I would more often than not be asked, "Is this business or personal?" It's no big surprise that when I actually knew the person and could answer "personal," the response would be more friendly and helpful. When I had to confess that it was for business, the reception was a bit more cold or, not coincidentally, businesslike. I didn't like the "business" response, and the results were never as good. It was too awkward.

I ultimately decided I was going to make every call personal in one way or another. I made a point of creating a relationship on some level with everyone who answered the phone. I had noticed that the more I reached out to others, the better the call went because people felt that they knew more about me. So, I began giving up little pieces of information about myself and, similarly, collecting little pieces of information about them. It wasn't anything major, just, you know, "I just got married, bought a house." This was just with the folks answering the phone—not even the person I needed to ultimately speak with. But it was obvious: the more they knew about me, the more they would be comfortable telling me stuff about themselves and about the person I was trying to connect with.

Providing personal information that allows folks to think of you in a positive light and feel closer to you on a personal level is *more* than okay. To forge unbreakable business relationships, you must get personal, at some level, with business contacts. The more they know about you, the more connected they will feel to you. I'm not suggesting that you take incredible risks and tell folks every intimate detail about yourself. However, there is a level of personal information that makes perfect sense and actually helps you obtain more business.

When I was running marketing for the Patriots, we spent a lot of time with clients, depending on how much we wanted the relationship to skew on a personal or business level. We were maniacal about the collection of information. Every exchange was an opportunity to extract any relevant detail that could assist us in building the relationship. We even attached every e-mail to each profile in the database to ensure that we understood all the nuances of the relationship.

Gathering information is probably the biggest tool you can use to build a business relationship, and the people who are exceptional at it know that they have to give if they are going to get. If you are to become a master gatherer, you have to not only do your due diligence in requesting information but also be willing to divulge of yourself as well.

5. Thou Shalt Not Stop Here

That's it: don't stop. Don't kill the relationship by not paying attention to it. Cultivate the discipline of applying the following commandments diligently.

6. Send Periodic Notes to Keep Communication Flowing

Stay on people's radar. The mechanism does not matter—e-mail, text, DM, BBM—just keep the conversation flowing. Murray Kohl, who worked for me at the Patriots and is now the vice president of sales for the team, used to compile news about the team from a variety of sources and send it to his distribution list every morning. It was the same information folks could get in the newspaper or on the Web, but Murray spent a little extra time in the morning to package it in a way that helped his clients (and potential clients) get information about the team. Most important, these messages made their recipients think of Murray. It was a very clever method of keeping himself at the top of his clients' minds. If they are thinking of you, they are more likely to do business with you. Find a vehicle that suits you and your relationships to keep the lines of communication open.

7. Surprise People by Remembering Something That Is Very Important to Them

Remembering things that are important to those you're solidifying connections with is an extremely powerful method of cementing a relationship, but it takes some serious time. You'll need to review the detailed profile information on the individual you plan on interacting with and surprise her. I happen to love surprising clients, so I have a bunch of fun stories that I'd love to share, but this one tops the list.

A few years ago, I was at a NASCAR race in Charlotte with one of our clients, Richard Childress Racing. We were in the pits prior to the race with our pals from RCR, Tom Knox and Jason Garrow, just shooting the breeze and getting ready for the race, when Tom and Jason spotted a couple of people they had done some promotions with. One of those people was Jean Beauvoir, the president of Renegade Nation. The RCR team introduced us to Jean, we hit it off immediately, and Jean requested a meeting.

In just a few weeks, we were headed to Renegade's offices.

Renegade Nation is Steven Van Zandt's company. You may know Steven as Little Steven from Bruce Springsteen's E Street Band or as Silvio from the HBO series *The Sopranos*. Our goal in the meeting was to convince those present (but specifically Steven) that TrinityOne should be Renegade's marketing arm and help utilize its brand to create revenue-generating extensions. At that time, we viewed the music business as a bit outside our realm, because it was, as we were born and bred in the sports industry. Although there are clear similarities between sports and music as entertainment, the reality at that time was that we were purely sports guys. Looking back on it, it's funny that our thoughts then were that sports marketing was only a niche and a specialty. Of course, we now realize that much of what we have learned and experienced in the sports business for nearly 25 years can be very effective tools for any business.

But the fact remains that, prior to this meeting, we viewed our chances as a stretch.

Because the music industry was a little outside of our wheelhouse, I asked the staff to really beef up the background information in the profiles that they were putting together. I wanted to get in there and really connect with Steven, and when you have something in common with the people you're talking to, it's clearly easier to converse.

So, there I sat on the plane heading out to the meeting, reviewing the profiles and trying to digest as much information as possible. Unfortunately, my head is not a computer, and there's only so much that I can absorb. To combat this, I have gotten into the practice of pulling out three tidbits of information, three little things that can potentially connect me with the person I'm speaking with. I always have a solid understanding of the whole, but it's helpful to focus on a few specific facts.

As I surveyed the profile, I noticed that one of Steven's right-hand people, John, happened to be a part of the production team for Aerosmith's "Love in an Elevator." Aerosmith is a Boston band, and for some reason I thought, "Maybe there's a connection and I can use this in the meeting. I'm from Boston and . . . Oh, I'll probably never meet this guy John." But it stuck in my brain.

Let's fast-forward.

We get to the meeting. I'm sitting down with Stevie and I'm pitching him, and he's into me. He's *getting* me. He's calling me the "Moneyman." He's kind of crazy and larger than life—in a good way. Like most athletes and entertainers, he's ultra creative and expressive. I'm becoming more comfortable because I know how to deal with athletes and owners, and I am now seeing Stevie in the same light. I'm giving him the whole spiel. I'm bringing him to the river of dreams; he's grabbing the bucket, ready to pick it up. He's excited by everything I am laying out for him, when all of a sudden, John walks by. Stevie calls out, "John, John, come here! You gotta meet Lou! Lou is the *Moneyman*!"

And there it is.

John comes over, and Stevie says, "Hey, this is John Luongo." And I respond, "John Luongo. That name sounds familiar . . . hmmm . . . Hey! You're the dude who produced 'Love in an Elevator'!"

Stevie almost dropped dead on the floor.

He was amazed that a sports guy would have a clue about who produced *any* song, never mind that his guy John had produced "Love in an Elevator." He looked at me bewildered and said, "How do you *know* that?"

My answer? "I'm the Moneyman. I *have* to know that."

"You're hired! You're hired!" shouted Stevie.

Something as silly as that (although I think we had the gig anyway) put him over the edge. That *little* tidbit sealed the deal.

When you can surprise people by knowing something that you have no reason to know or remember something that is important to a person, it resonates in a way that is much more powerful than just regurgitating the superficial stuff that everyone else probably knows, like what college she attended. Don't get me wrong, you need to know that too, as well as her husband's name, her kids' names, and so on—but nothing is more valuable than when you reveal those hidden jewels of information.

8. Invite People to an Event That You Can Attend Together

When I write that you should be inviting people to "events," I don't necessarily mean that you need to be chartering 10-day private Mediterranean cruises for you and your clients.

Not that there's anything wrong with that.

Attending events with people is valuable, whether they're as simple as a wine-tasting dinner or as dramatic as the Super Bowl. The magnitude doesn't matter, because with all of the intelligence you have gathered to this point about the individual, you know what the person likes and enjoys doing. In this particular commandment, the purpose is not to send the person and his family to an event; it's to spend time together to help seal the bond. Don't *give* him tickets to a ball game; *take* him to a ball game!

I need to be clear: too many people screw this step up, primarily because they are not paying attention to its purpose. You cannot miss out on this important piece of the relationship-building puzzle. Getting tickets for someone is *nice*, but it's not what this is about.

Through your fact finding from Commandment Four, identify an event that fits and go *together*. There is so much value in this, and it will help you expedite the process of building the relationship. Even if you have a large entertainment budget, don't get caught up in spending just to make an impression. Sometimes the simple things work just as well, provided they are thoughtful. The obvious thought you put into it will help you win the relationship.

9. See That What You Do DELIVERS to the Relationship

Since we spent an entire chapter on what DELIVERS entails, you get it, and it's already a part of you. Let this serve as a reminder that cultivating the DELIVERS mindset and approach is one major step in the entire process—a very big step that takes you from the minor leagues to the majors when it comes to building business relationships.

Here's a little tip that may help in the process. You know that you have to hit every letter of the DELIVERS acronym to make it come to fruition, so make a little game with the relationship you are building and tally how many letters you cover during each encounter. Then, the next time you interact with the same person, make sure you touch on other letters. If you do this on a habitual basis, you will find you are consistently delivering to relationships.

That word *consistently* leads me to the Tenth Commandment.

10. Repeat Commandments 6 through 9 on a Consistent Basis

These Ten Commandments just aren't a *one and done* proposition. You have to be diligent in repeating the process and adding new facets to evolve the relationship. If you don't continuously devote energy to its evolution, the relationship will become extinct. The only way to become great at building business relationships that lead to closing deals is practice, practice, practice.

Football teams practice for five days to prepare for one game. Bands practice every day for hours upon hours to be ready to play their weekend gig. So why, in everyday life, do people just fly by the seat of their pants?

I ask, because they do—every single day.

CREATING MEMORABLE MOMENTS

No matter what business you are in, it is your responsibility to separate yourself from your competitors. It's really as simple as that. Think about Macy's and Gimbel's, Coke and Pepsi, or Visa and Master-Card. In reality, there aren't monumental differences between each of these pairs of companies. Pepsi? It's just sugar, water, and cola flavor. Coke? Same thing: it's sugar, water, and cola flavor. Because many competitors are so close in reality, they need to engineer the *perception* of difference and either find or create a mechanism to put some distance between them and other competitive brands. They need an edge, something that separates them from the rest of the pack.

MEMORABLE MOMENTS

Individuals in business can face the same hurdles. How is one lawyer or accountant different from another? This can be even trickier for individuals because they do not have powerhouse agencies behind them to cue the smoke and mirrors. That doesn't mean they cannot create their own distinct features that separate them from the rest of the pack, however. Whether you're a company or an individual, the key is to create *memorable moments* that will be permanently ingrained in the minds of the individuals, consumers, business partners, or fans you are trying to impress. These indelible impressions you leave with others are the glue that makes you stick in their minds, not just for the moment, but also for the long haul.

When I was with the Patriots, we used to entertain a group of potential and existing partners at every game. We had an entire game-day agenda planned to ensure that the people we entertained would never forget the day they spent with us. When they arrived at the stadium, they would drive into a special parking lot, where a marketing representative would greet them; the rep would escort them up to our suite, where they would be wined and dined. We were always sure to balance the guests in the suite with an appropriate mixture of current and potential partners so that we weren't the only ones touting our organization, and typically we had a celebrity who would join us just to put the cherry on top of the Sunday. (Yeah, I spelled it right. We were football—it was Sunday.)

Every detail was carefully engineered. Prior to kickoff, we took our guests down to the sideline for pregame warm-ups. We made sure our guests were situated perfectly so that when we shot photographs with the owner, the players would be in the background of the frame. Just before the players lined up to be introduced at the start of the game, a select few guests, special sponsors, and people whom we were hoping to close for big money were escorted into the tunnel—a huge inflatable Patriots helmet—and positioned at the side of the entrance. At this point, the crowd in the stands was working itself into a frenzy, and the players started streaming into the tunnel, jumping up and down, slamming each other's pads within arm's reach of our guests. With the pump-up music blasting, the players getting fired up, and the crowd going nuts, the feeling of intensity in that helmet was indescribable.

At just the right moment, my director of entertainment, Gary Grodecki, would play some of *Carmina Burana*. A great Patriots video would be showing on the big screen, edited to the precise beat of the music that led into an amazing crescendo. You could see the goose bumps on the guests we brought into the helmet. I won't lie; I had them too. At this point, the crowd in the stands was deafening. We'd cue the song "Crazy Train," and Ozzy Osborne screamed, "ALL ABOARD!" Energy was at a fever pitch as the players shot out of the helmet, some of them hand-slapping our guests, who, at this point, had died and gone to sports fan heaven.

Voilà. A memorable moment.

No doubt. No question. By bringing a handful of people down onto the field, we created such an incredible memorable moment for our guests that there was no chance that they would ever forget our names or that experience . . . and just to underscore it, that week we sent them a framed photo from the day with a Patriots logo smack on the bottom of it. I promise you, we separated ourselves from the competition with that stunt. As you would imagine, our closure rate for those who had the helmet experience was dramatically higher than average. If you want to beat out your competitors, you need to create memorable moments.

The most important thing you have to understand about memorable moments, what you have to be absolutely clear about, is that you must be certain that you and the memory are one. That's a tall order.

I can already hear you saying, "But Lou, I don't have a huge Patriots helmet and players and . . ." Stop. Memorable does not equal magnitude. The memorable moments you create don't have to be as over the top as the experiences we were able to produce; it's not about the *helmet*. The key is to find a way to create memories in which your face, the moment, and your company's identity all stick in the recipient's mind. Even small gestures can be incredibly impactful if you are thoughtful and willing to get creative.

My dad was a master at designing great memorable moments. He was a pharmaceutical sales rep for Eli Lilly in the 1970s, and he was charged with calling on doctors and hospitals to convince them to use his company's particular products. At the time, Eli Lilly didn't have a monopoly on the drugs that the hospitals needed, and there was an incredible amount of competition for each hospital account. However, my dad was a tremendous Relationship Architect; he would build solid bonds not only with the doctors and nurses, but also with the administrators and assistants. He knew that the better the relationship he had with everyone in a doctor's office, the better his chances of closing the sale. He paid extra attention to the assistants and receptionist because he knew they were the gatekeepers to the folks who made the decisions.

My dad built relationships so solid that he would get calls from assistants saying, "Louie, they are swamped today, and they are never going to be able to break away for lunch." My dad would take that cue and go to Spinelli's in East Boston, pick up trays of Italian cold cuts, pasta, and chicken cutlet Parmesan, and head into the office a hero. He was notorious for bringing food to his clients at lunchtime when he knew they were too busy to run out to get a bite. Get this: not only would he bring lunch to them, but he would also lay it out, help serve it, and clean up. Once everything was set up in a conference room, the receptionist would page the physicians and say, "Louie Imbriano from Eli Lilly brought in food, and it's in the conference room. Come and get it." My dad would be behind the table serving everyone food. My dad's smile and a warm lunch on a day someone otherwise might not have eaten was genius. No Patriots helmet, no Ozzy, no pad-pounding players, but let me tell you, these hungry folks never forgot what he did.

Voilà. A memorable moment.

My dad's efforts gave him such an edge that those people who'd eaten Louie's lunch never forgot—even when they switched jobs. In fact, when my dad moved to Miles Laboratories (which became Bayer Pharmaceuticals), he was able to bring relationships with him from every position he'd held at Eli Lilly. I promise you, even without a sports team in your back pocket, you can start creating memorable moments like my dad did and separate yourself from your competitors. You'll walk away victorious, having won the customer.

Magnitude or Attitude?

Both the helmet and the hot lunch are successful memorable moments to the core. However, most people still get caught up in the importance of the magnitude of the event. In the memory-making business, the magnitude of the moment you're creating *does not in itself* guarantee that you'll be a part of the memory, which is essential. You don't need to incorporate one of the Seven Wonders of the World to make the moment memorable. If fact, sometimes the event and the moment are so overwhelming that you could get lost in the mix; if you get cut out of the memory, you've totally missed the point. The equation for creating memorable moments is less about pomp and circumstance and more about your forethought and how you make others feel in the process. This is a simple concept: it's all about your attitude and how you make people feel.

The beauty of this is that if you put forethought into your actions, the smallest effort will stand out in people's minds and make them think of you—and often. In the mid-1990s, I was in a steak restaurant in Boston doing a little entertaining. That evening, there was a special on the menu, seared tuna in a wasabi sauce. A few of us ordered the tuna, and when the dish arrived at the table, we tasted it, and we all felt that if it had a bit more soy sauce and wasabi, it would be perfect.

I mentioned this to the waiter, whom I now know as Jimmy, and asked if he could bring us some more soy and wasabi. Jimmy was quick to oblige, but when he returned a few moments later, he had the soy sauce but no wasabi and in its place an apology from the kitchen. They were out of wasabi.

Jimmy was great and incredibly apologetic. We went back to eating and chatting, then, after about five minutes, Jimmy came back with a bit of sweat on his brow and a container of wasabi. The table was delighted, and I said, "Oh, great, the kitchen found some." Jimmy replied, "No, they're still out, but I ran a couple of blocks down to the Japanese restaurant and they gave me some for you."

Voilà. Do I even need to say it? A memorable moment.

Do you think I remembered Jimmy at tip time? In fact, who do you think I asked for every time I went to the restaurant? When I recommended the restaurant to people, friends, clients, or anyone who mattered to me, I knew I could trust Jimmy to deliver incredible service.

Jimmy created a memorable moment that now, 15 years later, I still remember. The beauty of Jimmy's memorable moment was that he was just being himself and trying to do a great job for the patrons of the restaurant, but he made sure that our meal at his table and his face were chiseled in our minds. Jimmy is a Relationship Architect. That small, no-cost effort made as much of an impact as a major event might have—maybe even more. Jimmy wasn't consciously going out of his way to create a long-term relationship; he was just doing his job to the max. Was he working it for a plush tip? Absolutely, but so what? We all can learn a lot from the Jimmys of the world. Their can-do attitude is what separates them from the rest of the schmucks.

You can't have a can-do attitude only when money is on the line; you need to have one regardless of the situation if you want to stand out in the business of creating memorable moments. A group of us were in New York for my buddy Joey Limone's engagement party. We had all come into the city for the weekend, and there were a bunch of activities planned—dinners, cocktail parties, all of the festivities that go along with that kind of gig. The entire weekend had been scheduled up until Sunday morning. Everyone was heading back to his or her home base at different times, so that day was going to be a bit more ad hoc.

Although by that time we had been together for many years, it was the very first time my wife, Patricia, and I had been in New York City together. I wanted to do something special, so when we woke up on Sunday morning, I said to her, "The city is yours. We'll do whatever you want." She got an excited look on her face and mentioned that she had heard that Tavern on the Green was a special place to have brunch.

"Of course," I said. "No problem." I suggested we see if anyone else wanted to join us and asked her to buzz the restaurant to get a table for 2 p.m. My buddies Steve Szymanski and Ricky LeBlanc were still in town and, although the thought of food was enticing, the two bachelors were on the fence about going to Tavern on the Green. To be honest, Tavern on the Green is a little foofy for me and my crew, but it's what Patricia wanted.

Patricia called Tavern on the Green and said that she would like to make a reservation. The person on the other end asked, "When would you like the reservation?" Patricia proceeded to tell her 2 p.m. There was a pause on the other end, and then a curt chuckle, followed by, "Madame, this is *the* Tavern on the Green; we are booking reservations for three months from now." Patricia hung up, obviously disappointed, and said that our brunch plans would have to change—Tavern on the Green was booked solid for three months.

I told her to get ready anyway and to tell the boys we were heading over around 1-ish. I jumped in the shower while she rang up Steve and Ricky. While I was getting dressed, I asked Patricia if the boys were in. She said, "Oh, yeah, I told them the restaurant was booked solid and that you said we were heading there anyway. They said they weren't in the mood for a fancy brunch but they wouldn't miss this for the world."

The four of us jumped into a cab and headed to Tavern on the Green.

When we got there, we entered the foyer, where everyone was waiting to be seated. I navigated through the sea of people, my crew of three in tow, up to the reservation desk. The maître d', who was all business, asked for my name. "Franklin," I answered. He looked up and down the list and said, "I'm sorry, sir, I do not see a Franklin on our list. Could your reservation be under another name?" While sliding him a c-note, I said, "You must be missing it. Table for four. Franklin, Ben Franklin." The pretentious dude looked up at me and said, "Oh, yes, Mr. Franklin, wait one moment." I smirked at my crew and gave them the nod. We were in.

A moment later, my new best friend looked over and said, "Right this way to the Crystal Room, sir." As we followed him, we saw four waiters carrying in a table, chairs—the whole setup. They plopped the table in the middle of the room, and instantly everything was arranged as though they'd been waiting for hours for our arrival. The maître d' told us to enjoy our brunch. Most important, Patricia, Steve, and Ricky were enjoying every aspect of the scene—I was creating a memorable moment *for them*.

You might be saying, "Lou, sure, when you have money, it's easy to wave it around and get what you want." But this is the truth: creating memorable moments and eliciting the response you want is more about having the proper attitude and owning a situation than anything else. At the time, we actually had no business going to the Tavern on the Green, never mind slipping the host $100. I worked in radio and made little money, and we had just bought our first house. But my philosophy has always been to capture moments like that—they're to be seized and enjoyed. After all, it was our first time in New York City together, and Patricia never asks for anything. I wasn't going to let a little thing like a reservation bring her any disappointment. Besides, missing an opportunity like that for practical reasons is sure to turn into a future regret—and regrets are not what you want embedded in a memorable moment.

THE BOW

Your attitude is your biggest asset when you're creating memorable moments. The proper attitude can get you far, but in order to fully capitalize on the moment, you need to proactively direct the creation process. Every successful memorable moment will have evidence of each of these: forethought, preparation, creativity, timing, pertinence, and attitude. The best memorable moments, though, include what I like to call "the Bow."

You might remember that I mentioned Michael O'Hara Lynch, my bud from Visa, in Chapter 5. If you are in the sports marketing or banking world, you know Mike. He is a legendary Relationship Architect who is a master of the art of creating memorable moments. I promise you, you want to be like Mike. I met him at the turn of the century when I was with the Patriots. Michael and I negotiated the deal between the team and Visa, which I believe is still a part of the team's portfolio.

Over the years, I have learned a lot about the elements of successful memorable moments from Mr. O'Hara Lynch. In fact, he introduced me to a few key ingredients of memorable moments that produce nothing less than magic. You'll certainly want to incorporate these ideas into your own thinking. I once joined Michael at the Daytona 500; it's the crown jewel of all NASCAR races, and I'm sure it's included on many people's bucket lists.

As a participant and a guest of Michael's and Visa's, I have to tell you that the precision of their planning prior to the event was amazing. Michael and his team had every detail covered from start to finish. He set up the group at Disney World, away from the jammed streets of Daytona, and the agenda included plush lunches, dinners, parties, park tickets—all the bells and whistles. The day before the race, Michael's crew took the entire group to the Richard Petty Experience at Disney so that everyone could take a couple of laps in a real stock car on an authentic track. While we were suiting up and getting ready for a thrill of a lifetime, one of the drivers whom Visa was sponsoring at the time, Kurt Busch, showed up to chat with us, take photos, and give us pointers for when we took the wheel. Michael was there in the middle of all the action telling the driver, "Hey, Kurt, come over here and say hello to my pal Lou."

This trip had all the ingredients for the great elements of memorable moments: forethought, preparation, creativity, pertinence, timing, and attitude. However, this next, small piece is what made the moment, and Michael, memorable. The trip included an unexpected treat, what I've started calling the Bow, and I found it when I entered my room just after checking in. You might expect the most special moment of the experience to be at a big event, like the race, the meet and greet, or on the track in the stock car, but it wasn't. When I walked into the room, the message light was blinking. I wasn't expecting any messages—after all, I'd just checked in. I picked up the receiver, logged into the voice mail, and heard: "Hi, this is Rusty Wallace [the driver for the #2 car at the time], and I would like to welcome you to your trip with Visa to the Daytona 500." Rusty then proceeded to wish us an enjoyable trip and threw in a few details about what we could expect over the next few days.

Voilà. Another memorable moment.

That 30 seconds was magical, and I wasn't even a NASCAR or Rusty Wallace fan. It was magical because of its simplicity and the forethought it communicated to me as a guest. That short message indicated to everyone in attendance that he could rest assured that *every* detail had been handled and that we were in good hands: it was the Bow to wrap up the entire package.

I call it the Bow because a bow is as simple as a little strip of ribbon, but once it is wrapped just right around a package, it ties everything together and makes it perfect.

Think about when you get a present for your birthday or during the holidays. When you get gifts at those times, you're almost *expecting* the gift—just as I was expecting to have a great time at Mike's events. While you're always excited about gifts, even if you're expecting them, when they are thoughtfully wrapped with care and a spectacular bow, it just makes the gift feel that much more special. A bow makes a great present that much better, because it's not about the gift or the possession, but about the thought put into it. The Bow solidifies the moment and the memory.

I don't care how tough you are or how rigid you may be, when someone takes the time and effort to make what is important to you even more special, she and that memory will be indelible in your mind. So when I checked into the room, even though there was a bag of cool swag, that 30-second message let me know that Michael and Visa cared about my enjoyment and were going to make sure that they had everything covered.

Of course, as soon as I got back to the stadium and we began drawing up our plans for the upcoming year with our own clients, I borrowed Michael's concept, and we added a welcome message to our team trip experiences. I also began preaching to my staff about what an impact the Daytona 500 trip had on me, all of which came directly from Michael's attention to detail. My staff and I became committed to finding the Bow for everything we did, and we're challenging you to do the same. If you change your thinking, you'll realize just how easy it is to find the Bow that builds relationships and wins the customer.

Finding the Bow and Tying It Perfectly

Now that we've discussed the importance of *attitude* over *magnitude* and the need for the Bow on every package, let's talk about exactly how to successfully identify the Bow in any memorable moment. I would love to tell you that there is a science to finding the Bow, but as with most aspects of Relationship Architecture, including the right Bow is an art form that requires practice. That being said, we're not going to leave you without a sense of direction. When you are in search of the Bow for your memorable moment, you have to think of it as an unexpected treat; it's all about the emotional play. The tangible aspects of the item or concept are totally secondary. Here's where creativity, pertinence, and timing play a significant role.

Let's start simply. Imagine that you're in charge of putting on a global managers' meeting for your company at a resort in the Caribbean. You're planning a beachside event that includes a dinner, a speaking program, and a few other activities. The theme of the event is "Let Loose," so when your guests arrive, they find on their assigned seats a pair of flip-flops in their size in a bag emblazoned with the company's logo. That's an unexpected treat. Their unexpectedness makes the whole event a bit more special and memorable. That small gesture sticks in the minds of the guests.

As we said, it's a simple idea. It's easy. Anyone could come up with flip-flops. Understanding *why* it's such a good idea is the point here: the gesture is *pertinent* to the trip and the theme, the *timing* of its delivery makes it stand out, and although it's a simple gift, it has a flair of *creativity*—flip-flops don't have much to do with the boardroom your guests usually meet in.

While the idea is pretty simple, the truth is that the key to all of this is not the idea itself; it's all about the planning and execution. That's where most memorable moments get lost in the shuffle. Prior to the trip and its events, the organizers had to have the forethought to include this Bow, knowing full well that each treat is what makes the trip stick in the minds of all who attended. The skill lies in understanding what it takes to make the smallest gestures come to life.

It's All about the Execution

Those flip-flops didn't just appear magically on the individuals' seats the night of the event. After coming up with the concept, the detail work followed; people had to secure a vendor, select a flip-flop design, and include shoe size in the form that participants filled out prior to the trip. (When prepping for trips at the Patriots, we had a standard form for each guest that, in addition to the standard "King or Double" and "Smoking or Non-Smoking" checkboxes, included shirt size, shoe size, allergies, and so on.) After the planners had gathered the info, they had to have the flip-flops produced, order additional pairs in varying sizes in case the size given was inaccurate in some way, have pairs available for folks who did not provide the info requested (this happens *all* the time), and *actually place each pair of flip-flops on the right seat with the right place card.* This isn't difficult stuff, but the number of dotted i's and crossed t's required to nail it is enough to throw planners off course.

The simple concept is suddenly not so simple; like all great ideas, it requires some serious backend work to bring it all to life. No idea is great unless it can be pulled off with perfection.

The Hunt for the Perfect Bow

My staff and I are constantly on the lookout not only for events that can use that extra touch, but also for information that can help us thrill individuals one at a time. We are always asking questions, probing to find out more about the people we come in contact with, which leads us to brainstorming, planning, and execution. If we know that a particular individual likes a specific beverage or has a hobby that is dear to him, it leads us to that Bow for the individual.

One of our smaller clients at the Patriots was a Jack Daniels drinker, and *every* time he was with us, he would order a "Jack and Coke." He traveled with us sometimes, and we decided to do something a little extra for him. On one team trip, he got to his room and, like every other guest, found a swag bag. But his bag was special—we had tucked in a bottle of Jack Daniels and a bottle of Pepsi (we were a Pepsi team, so we had to be true to our sponsor).

EXTRA POINTS
Staying true to your sponsors sends a great message to
people with whom you're still building relationships.
It communicates to them that you'll stay just as loyal
to them as your relationship solidifies.

Naturally, our guest was thrilled, and over the course of the next few years, he became one of our larger sponsors, dancing around the seven-figure level. I'm certainly not suggesting that the bottle of Jack in his bag was what compelled him to graduate to a higher level of spending, but here's what it *did* do: when we called, he picked up the phone. He was always quick to mention that we had the JD waiting for him. The Bow we'd given him loosened up our relationship with him and compelled him to be more available for new opportunities. The key thing to remember here is that what we did wasn't just wining and dining. Anyone can do that. We showed him that we valued him enough to pay attention to what was important to him and cared enough to go that extra step. *That's* what's going to separate you from the others and the competition. The Bow is crucial to getting you to the next level of marketing.

On the flip side, if you totally space out on those details, it could blow up in your face. Let's go back to the game-day entertaining we did each week in our marketing suite. It probably goes without saying that this was a tremendous opportunity to build relationships, and we were quite effective at it. The suite would always have a mixture of current clients, potential clients, and a special celebrity guest or two. We made sure that we didn't have guests from competing companies at the same game or in the same sponsorship category. While both DIRECTV and Comcast were sponsors of the game, there was no need to send mixed messages to either company, and they probably didn't need to be hanging out together on a Sunday afternoon.

One Sunday we invited some people from Welch's, which was not a sponsor, up to the suite, and we hit every item on the checklist: no one from Ocean Spray or Pepsi was invited to the suite that day, we ordered the fridge stocked with Welch's juices, and we planned to keep a few Ocean Spray bottles on the shelves because Ocean Spray is a sponsor and this underscored our message of loyalty. Well, game day rolled around, all was going well, we opened the fridge to offer our Welch's guests a drink, and BAM: nothing but Ocean Spray products.

The staff in food and beverage had hung us out to dry. It wasn't their fault, though, because the execution on our part shouldn't have ended with placing the order; it was our responsibility to follow up and double-check, which obviously we had not done. Needless to say, we did not place ourselves in the best light with that blunder. While Welch's was not a sponsor and Ocean Spray was, you have to remember that the people from Welch's were guests in our house, and our mission was to make them feel comfortable. Let me say that again: as a Relationship Architect, the fact that Ocean Spray is a corporate sponsor is *irrelevant* to how you treat the folks at Welch's, especially when they are invited to your suite.

Unfortunately, bad memorable moments don't pack the same punch as a great memorable moment—they're usually worse, and the negative impression is sometimes hard to recover from. The amount of work required to regain that positive feeling is 10 times the amount of the effort required to do it right in the first place. Needless to say, we were not getting a Welch's deal anytime soon, and we had some work to do.

GROUPS: EXPONENTIALLY MAGNIFIED RELATIONSHIPS

I mentioned earlier that Michael O'Hara Lynch has been instrumental in my understanding and embracing of the Bow. Mike introduced me to a couple of things that were particularly magical, the first of which was the Rusty Wallace message in our suite that greeted us on the Daytona 500 trip. Here's the second: every year Michael hosts a "Partners Conference" to which Visa invites its partners from teams, leagues, and agencies to discuss Visa's initiatives and campaigns and to encourage the attendees to brainstorm on behalf of Visa. The folks in attendance are all VPs and C-level executives from the NFL, the Olympics, NASCAR, and so on. I think it's easy to see the value of holding a conference like this, but as a business-building opportunity and a relationship solidification mechanism, it was absolutely brilliant. The way Visa set everything up magnified and expedited the process of developing Relationship Architecture. Imagine taking everyone who loves you, putting them all in the same place, and treating them not only like kings and queens but like they are the only people that matter in the world. Powerful.

The first year I went to this Partners Conference, it was at Pebble Beach, a spectacular setting and location regardless of whether or not you play golf. As you would imagine, everything was organized with incredible attention to detail. Michael's group paid attention to *everything*. The room, the swag bag, gifts, golf, dinners . . . everything you could imagine was available—and then some.

But by now you should know that with Michael, there's going to be a pièce de résistance, and this one was incredible. One night after dinner, the whole group was invited to walk out to the seventeenth hole at the Pebble Beach Golf Course; once we were there, we discovered that the hole had been set up for a nighttime closest-to-the-pin contest. It was an incredible sight. Glow-in-the-dark rings created a bull's-eye right at the hole, and the flag was illuminated. The tee box was set up with a bar, tables, and chairs, and each person in the group took shots at hitting a glow-in-the-dark ball closest to the pin. We were so excited to be there that the game itself felt like a playoff match, with everyone cheering on the person in the tee box. The atmosphere produced such an incredible, unique experience. How many folks can say they had a glow-in-the-dark closest-to-the-pin contest on the seventeenth hole at Pebble Beach?

The brilliance of the entire trip wasn't the experience itself; it was the tight bond that Michael knew would develop among all of the attendees. The atmosphere bred closeness among the guests such that when we were in brainstorming sessions, everyone felt both comfortable with one another and as though she had a vested interest in Visa's success. The Bow, in this case, connected each of us *to each other*. Many of us continue to stay in touch, and when we chat, that Pebble Beach experience quite often comes up—we were always thinking about how we could work *together* and *include Visa*. We were the folks who were making the decisions for the team, and, while I can't speak for all of us, I know a good many of us would always have helping Visa in mind. Of course, Visa was a major sponsor of the Patriots, so we should have been thinking about helping Visa regardless, but truthfully, building relationships helps move reality toward what *should be* but doesn't always necessarily happen without some coaxing.

Relationship Architecture is about creating and leveraging people and relationships for everyone's good, and Michael and the Visa team knew how to create relationships and leverage sponsorships like nobody else. They had all the best minds in sports thinking about how they could help the Visa brand. So, so smart.

Relationships Equal Revenue

Relationship Architecture between individuals is an incredibly powerful tool, but when you apply the art form to groups, it amplifies what you've built exponentially. Relationship Architecture within a group is so dynamic because not only are your guests feeling how solid your relationship with them is, they are also telling each other how great you are, and *that* affirmation is magic. In Visa's case, the team engineered it so that there were dozens of high-level sports executives telling each other how great Visa is. That's why it's brilliant.

What's beautiful is that it's not as if the people on the Visa team weren't being genuine, because they absolutely were. They weren't trying to pull the wool over anyone's eyes. They just wanted to show us how much they cherished the relationship they had with each of us—and our organizations—and by doing so in a sincere way, they created solid relationships in an incredibly short period of time.

The practice of Relationship Architecture is a game changer in business. Of course you can get things done and experience success through smarts and hard work, but you magnify everything you do and accomplish so much more by taking the approach that every relationship is imperative and important. When we were building the new stadium and working on expanding our revenue, I would tell everyone in the organization, from top to bottom, "We can never have enough friends thinking about how they can help us." The *only* way to achieve that is to continually find ways to help *them*.

When I left the Patriots, I gave the Kraft family a year's notice. I didn't have a contract, and I had no obligation to do so. I just felt that I had been with them for close to a decade, and I wanted to show them how much I appreciated the opportunity they had afforded me to achieve great things with my arm of the organization. They were the ones who were taking all the risk and bankrolling every aspect of the team, so it felt impossible to leave them hanging. Furthermore, I left only after I asked Jonathan multiple times if he and the Kraft family wanted to start a sports marketing company.

Giving a year's notice threw off my own planning for the future and altered how I proceeded with my new company, but I felt it was the only way to depart. I know many people think that I just up and left because I didn't talk about it publicly until the very end. But I believe giving 12 months' notice will always separate me from almost any other employee of theirs and make a statement to every other organization I work with.

It's important to remember that exceptional Relationship Architecture is not about creating grand opportunities like being on the field and high-fiving the players as they are introduced. It's not just about feeding people and entertaining folks and giving them gifts. It's not just about finding the Bow.

The reality is, Relationship Architecture is all about thinking ahead, paying attention to the relationship, and continually considering what will strengthen it. There is no formula. Two ball games, three expensive dinners, and six mentions of their kids does not guarantee that you will have a remarkable business relationship. Relationship Architecture is not a science; it is an art that you have to hone and practice over the course of time.

YOUR NETWORK, NOT YOUR NET WORTH

If you do take the approach we describe in this section and practice, practice, practice, you cannot help but become an exceptional Relationship Architect. The practice will allow you to build a portfolio of relationships, which can only fuel your success. After all, being a success is not about an individual, but about those people who surround that individual. As you look back, you'll see that the relationships you forged over the years will be a true test of your success.

Someone may have titles and money, but if you want to pinpoint a successful person, evaluate the strength and numbers of a person's relationship portfolio. Success is not fueled by one's *net worth*; it's driven by one's *network*, a network that leads to revenue generation for you and your company.

THE REVENUE GAME

CONVERTING RELATIONSHIPS INTO REVENUE

Once your business has been structured to execute seamlessly, you understand your customers and how to create promotions that they'll love, and you're an expert at building relationships, you're *still* not done if you want to become a consistent revenue-generating machine. It's entirely possible to have all of the above and still not have what it takes to close deals.

In this section, we're going to look at the nuts and bolts of the sales process. We'll show you how to engage with companies and individuals to allow you to get *the* meeting (instead of being the guy who goes straight to voice mail and never gets a call back). We'll talk about how to bring your clients through the new business funnel to ensure that you get results. You don't want to waste time exploring impossible prospects; we're going to show you how to find ones with real possibility.

Successful closers have common traits that you can cultivate in yourself. We'll outline these important traits and then teach you how you can begin to implement them. We'll also spend time looking at what might be the most important thing we have to offer: stories and examples of how things go wrong, why it's easy to shy away from being a great salesperson, why potential consumers and partners balk at doing business with you, and how to head off disaster as much as possible.

Let's not waste time.

BUILD, DON'T SELL

OK, let's get to the good stuff: generating revenue. All of the principles and philosophies laid out in *Winning the Customer* up to this point are for the purpose of making money. Yes, that's right, making money. I said it, and I'm not ashamed that I did. The reason you're in business is to make a profit, and no matter what strategy you implement, you cannot lose sight of that endgame. The key is to do it the right way and to understand that relationships equal revenue. All of the effort you'll expend to create an efficient structure and implement the steps required to become a great Relationship Architect is specifically aimed at utilizing those relationships you built to lead your organization to revenue growth and long-term sustainability. The problem is that most folks think that making money is just about asking for the sale and being a closer. While being able to close is a crucial part of the process, focusing solely on closing can lead an individual and a company astray.

STOP SELLING

There are too many organizations that are focused solely on selling in order to generate revenue. I hear stories all the time of salespeople who make cold calls and try to get someone to buy their products or services during the first exchange. Please stop. This type of approach is archaic, and it insults the person you are chatting with. Spam is spam, regardless of the method by which it is delivered—via the Internet, phone, regular mail, or even in person. So stop selling. Strike that word from your vocabulary, because in business, it can be a dirty word.

The products and services you offer are a means to recognize revenue, but they are not what you should pitch. Instead, you should be introducing *yourself* and what you stand for—or, in the case of a company, its brand and what it stands for. Fundamentally, there is way too much competition in any given industry for you to focus purely on the items you offer. If you're really honest, most of the items and services your company offers are comparable to, if not exactly the same as, what your competitors are selling.

EXTRA POINTS

If your company holds a monopoly because of a patent, you may think you have a case for operating in a more product-oriented fashion, but I still would not recommend it, because the likelihood is that you will have a competitor at some point in the future. Regardless of your industry or the number of competitors you have, you must address your customers in such a way that they want to do business with you regardless of how good your competitors' products and services are.

My pal Nick Varano, a Boston celebrity restaurateur, is a master of this concept. When you go into his restaurant, Strega, Nick is there with a big smile and a welcoming hug. He walks around the restaurant chatting with everyone, making each guest feel at home. The more he chats with customers and walks around the restaurant, the more he learns about his customers' likes and dislikes. Nick is an unbelievable Relationship Architect because he invests time in each of his patrons and makes a visit to his restaurant a personal experience. Nick makes a brief encounter with him evoke the feeling that you have been friends with him since childhood. He has an unbelievable knack for making people return to the restaurant and spend more often—the all-important frequency and volume we discussed earlier in the book. Most of his repeat customers come back to Strega because of Nick and how he made them feel; sure, the food is great, but the menu isn't what's driving their behavior.

How do I know? If you've never been to the North End of Boston, you need to know that it's *packed* with Italian restaurants, each one as good as the next. So, if you owned a restaurant on Hanover Street in the middle of the North End, how could you compete? The only way to get people to dine in your restaurant and spend money with you instead of with the dozens of other restaurants around you is to give them something they can't get in the other restaurants. The genius of what Nick does is that no other restaurant has what he offers: himself. Every handshake, every smile, every dessert sent to a table is a move that closes future business. *Never* will he say, "Why don't you get the new pasta?" or, "Buy this bottle of wine." Without asking for business, he gets business. The part that should excite you as a businessperson is that, like Marty (the owner of my corner store) and me, Nick never studied marketing. He's from East Boston like we are, so maybe it's just something in the water, but it's more likely that his success stems from his total lack of gimmicks. His day-to-day work is devoid of strategic selling techniques. Nick just understands how to make people feel welcome and comfortable in his restaurant. That genuine approach is what closes business.

If you approach your business in such a way that the quality your customers see is in you and your brand—as opposed to a list of the inventory you have to offer—then you will be positioned for sustainability and growth over the long haul. You cannot get trapped by the idea that simply because your product and services are better, customers will naturally prefer your products and services. Although the quality of your product is very important, the reality is that you and your word are the most important aspect of your success. "Products" are actually secondary to your business.

Don't get me wrong, if you have a bad product, how great a Relationship Architect you are becomes totally irrelevant: folks will *not* be making the purchase. But if your product is close to your competitors' or only slightly behind, the efforts you put forth to make potential customers believe in you and your brand will be the difference that wins and *keeps* their business.

Keep the Contract in the Drawer

I always say to people that my handshake is better than any legal, binding contract out there. Not only do I say so, but I live and breathe it. Contracts are a necessity in the world we live in, but once they're fully executed, the paperwork should go in a file and you should perform at the highest level, well beyond expectations, regardless of the contract's terms. If you consistently deliver at this level, you will earn credibility and trust.

Let's pick this up at the point of a fully executed contract. Your company and its new client reach an agreement about what it can provide the client that will help him do business. The contract is negotiated and signed. At this moment, both parties should put the contract in a drawer and never take it out again until it's time to renew the deal. I am a firm believer that once a client becomes a part of your family of partners, nitpicking over the contract should not be a part of the process. Yes, you should have a list of deliverables that you are obligated to provide—that should go without saying. But to me, that's where the deliverables begin, not where they end.

Too many folks get caught up in, "You bought these assets or services," and that's *that*. Guess what? You sell services and assets to recognize revenue, but *it's your job to make sure your client is accomplishing its goals* and actually doing business. If that means doing things that are outside the scope of the deal, then make damn sure you are doing just that.

Now, I'm not saying that you have to spend a lot of extra money or give away additional valuable assets that prevent you from making money for your company. What *does* need to happen is the creation of a real working partnership that helps your clients achieve their goals without negatively affecting yours. To do this, you need to create a fluid situation, characterized by working together to make things happen. Sometimes that may mean giving a little extra time, service, or assets. Other times, the extra bit that is needed will involve additional expense, and your client has to realize that some extras do cost a little more. Yes, it's OK after a contract is signed to present other opportunities or adjustments that could involve additional expenses for your client.

The key to doing that effectively, though, is open communication and the development of complete trust that you will do everything in your power to accomplish your customers' goals. Then, if something causes costs to increase, your client knows you are being straight with him. Trust and credibility between you and your client are crucial. If you create this fluidity within a deal, you'll find that it not only benefits your client but also positively affects you in multiple ways.

This reminds me of a time when I was with the Patriots and I reached out to one of the many sponsors with whom we had this type of relationship. I called John Holloran, who ran all of Pepsi's marketing initiatives with the team, and reported that we were kicking off a new initiative at the team, and I needed his support. Now, Pepsi was already a top-level sponsor that spent seven figures with the Patriots. I'm sure that if you just looked at it on paper and didn't understand the depth of the relationship, you'd find no legitimate reason for Pepsi to spend extra dollars with us.

In fact, in and of itself, this particular new initiative made little business sense for Pepsi and its goals. I absolutely knew this, and I didn't pretend otherwise. I began the conversation, "Hey, John, I need your help. We are kicking off this new initiative that is important to the team as we expand into this area. *It will not help you achieve any of your goals*, but I could use your support and $100,000." I'm paraphrasing, but I'm serious. I'm sure I went into more detail, but the point is that without hesitation, Mr. Holloran said, "You got it." No hesitation, no question; he was in. Why? He knew that we would be there in the same way for him and his brand at a moment's notice, just as we had been in the past—we always kept the contract in the drawer.

This is the ultimate goal for your relationship with as many clients as possible. I am pleased to say that we had that relationship with many of our sponsors and clients. Not all, but as you have probably found, some folks just don't get it and are contract technicians. I promise you, if you are a prisoner of the contract (that is, "Let's see what the contract says"), rest assured, both you and the client are definitely not getting the most out of the deal or your partnership.

I know that if we called John right now and asked him if the extra $100,000 was worth it, without hesitation, he would confirm that it was—frankly, I know this because I actually called him and asked if he minded me putting this story in the book. We strived to build fluid deals like that one that helped all of us work together to accomplish each other's goals. Again, the best way to initiate these types of relationships is to be up-front and direct with your clients.

This is not only the case with business-to-business partners; the same is true in a business-to-customer relationship. Even if you do not have contracts with your customers, by doing business with them, you create an unwritten obligation to help them achieve their goals. You are not in business to sell products to customers, and you shouldn't look at it that way. You too are in the business of finding solutions for your customers. That should be your unwritten rule of doing business and how you should serve them.

FORGOING THE SHORT-TERM SALE

One day in late summer, I was at my lake house, and I asked my wife if she wanted to go on a boat ride with the kids. She declined, saying that she couldn't because she was making gravy for Sunday dinner and she had to watch it to make sure it didn't burn. I suggested she turn down the heat and put a diffuser underneath it—after all, we would only be out for an hour. She said she needed a new diffuser and was having a hard time finding one.

Fast-forward to the middle of the next week: I was in Boston for a meeting, walking in Copley, when I passed a Williams-Sonoma store. I remembered that Patricia needed the diffuser, so I swung back to see if Williams-Sonoma carried them. I asked one of the store clerks if they had diffusers. "Of course," she said, and went to the back room to get me a couple. I was waiting happily, thrilled that the store had them and that I had remembered, when the clerk returned and informed me that they were out of stock. Without skipping a beat, she told me that I should go to Shaw's because she remembered seeing them there the last time she was shopping.

This was awesome: the woman was prioritizing helping me and solving my problem instead of trying to sell me another product that the store offered, like an extra-large $90 skillet. She could have said, "Buy this skillet! It'll accomplish the same thing as a diffuser." But no, she provided a solution that cost her company a sale—and, by doing so, she gained a customer.

I don't normally shop for kitchenware, and it was an aberration that I went in for the diffuser. As luck would have it, a month later we were at my buddy Snax's ski house, and he told me that he needed to buy new pots for the place. He invites us up all the time—basically every weekend—so I said, "Don't buy them. We'll get them for you." Guess where I went to buy a new set of pots. Of course: Williams-Sonoma—all because the sales clerk didn't try to sell me something else when the store didn't have a diffuser. If you've ever purchased a nice set of pots and pans, you know that they're not cheap—a lot more expensive than the cost of a diffuser. The sales clerk's choice *not* to sell made the difference—the difference that made me come back. Never let the short-term sale jeopardize a long-term customer commitment to your company.

Listen and Solve

The best approach that any new businessperson can develop is to listen to the needs of her customers and clients and look for ways to provide solutions to their problems. If the product or service that you offer does not fit with a prospect's goals, never repackage it to try to sell it to him anyway. That may lead to a short-term close and making your number for the month, but it will most definitely blow up a long-term relationship. If what you have to offer does not fit with the person or the company you are pitching, then say so. Be real. Tell him that it obviously isn't a right fit at this time, and that it would be a mistake to pretend it is. Operating within a faulty framework is no way to start doing business together. If you're truthful at the outset, there will be opportunities with the client in the future.

Obviously the *close* is imperative if you are to earn a living and generate revenue, but money will come if you are constantly building relationships. Don't focus on extracting money from a relationship; focus on *delivering*. You may have heard the phrase "A.B.C.!"—it's prevalent in the world of sales, and it was made famous by the David Mamet play *Glengarry Glen Ross*. It stands for "Always Be Closing." In the movie version, Alec Baldwin takes over managing a sales group and delivers a grand speech about a new sales contest. The first-place salesperson wins a Cadillac, the second-place salesperson wins a set of steak knives, and the third-place salesperson gets fired. He uses this intimidation tactic to introduce the ABCs of sales, declaring that great salespeople should Always Be Closing. It makes for an exciting scene, but its premise is, in reality, totally misleading. In fact, A.B.C. should really stand for "Always

Be Creating." Always be creating opportunities for your clients. Always be creating relationships. Always be creating credibility.

ALWAYS BE CREATING

When I was in radio, the general manager of my station was a great dude named John Maguire. When John talked about closing business, he would say, "It's our job to be the Money Zamboni and clean up all the cash on the table." In order to do that, you can't just sell people what you have; you have to be the conduit for what your customers need. Radio stations and media have the ability to be creative and assist clients in ways that go well beyond selling them radio commercials. While the same is true for sports teams, creating opportunities for your clients to do more business with you, really cleaning up all the cash on the table, is more than possible for any company that's not just focused on the inventory it has.

One night Joe Mariani, the director of sales at the Patriots, and I were having dinner with one of our partners, John O'Connor from GlaxoSmithKline. We had created a number of hospitality programs with John to help him achieve his goals, and he was spending a few hundred thousand with us, but we knew that his budget was deeper and that there was real potential for growth. Again, it was our job to be the Zamboni, which is not a bad thing, by the way. We were charged with generating more revenue for the team, so it was our job to extract as much money as possible from a client's budget. Don't lose sight of the point: generating revenue and cleaning up the money is great. Focusing on it and trying to "sell" just isn't the way to do so. We knew that going after GlaxoSmithKline's budget regardless of the outcome on its end would be bad business. But that wasn't the case at all: we wanted more of John's budget, and we were prepared to ensure that it would be better spent with us than with one of our competitors. It's your job to get more money out of clients, but do it the right way.

So, we were having this nice dinner and asking John a lot of questions; obviously, his answers should have been showing us how to create more for him. Midway through dinner, John told us that he loved the Patriots golf tournament and that it was very effective for him with his clients. He confessed that he wished he could get more foursomes. We asked if budgeting was a problem, and he responded that he could buy 18 if they were available. Ding, ding, ding! Joe looked at me, and I turned to John and said, "What if we created another tournament that is exclusive to GlaxoSmithKline?" John said, "Put something together that makes sense, and we're in." Start up the Zamboni!

The next day Joe and I sat down and discussed what we would need in order to accomplish John's goals and pull off another tournament. We had been doing a Patriots golf tournament around mini camp in June for a few years that was very successful, and John always bought three or four foursomes. The problem with getting a second tournament off the ground was that attending the first tournament was mandatory for all the players. We would place a player in each foursome, and the remaining players would be at holes or driving around in golf carts—if you were a fan and a golfer, you were in utopia for the day. Getting the players to attend a second tournament would be difficult, so we were going to have to find a mechanism to allure them.

We started planning, and we decided that the best way to make this a great day for John and his clients was to limit the event to 18 foursomes. If you have ever been in a tournament with 30 or more foursomes, you know how bogged down they can get and how long a day it can become. The beauty of this, though, was that we needed only 18 players. Joe had a contact at Ping, and one of my other guys, Will McDonough, had one at FootJoy, so the two went out and did deals to get full sets of clubs, bags, and shoes for the players and coaches who would be joining us for this extra day.

We planned the tournaments so that one was the day before mini camp and the other was the day after, so we knew the players would be in town. Then we gauged the players' interest and made sure it worked with the course, Willowbend. Once we had a complete plan, we went back to John with our proposal and a hefty price tag—as you would imagine—but with extreme value. John was thrilled, and we closed the deal in about 10 minutes. That tournament, in conjunction with its marketing contract for the year, got Glaxo's spending close to seven figures. It was a win/win deal all around, because if you provide value and solutions, you'll close new money. Always Be Creating.

Let's look more carefully at the process of creating the golf tournament for our client. It had three key ingredients: structure, information, and relationship, which perfectly illustrate how they led to revenue generation. Without a solid relationship with John, we could never have had the honest discussion that let us find out what he needed to achieve his goals. Once we had that information, we had what we needed to create a solution, *but* without a great marketing operational structure, we would never have been able to execute this initiative at the same time as all the other obligations we had on our plate. Each piece must work together for true upside to occur, and it's the shortsightedness that ignores the need for all three of these ingredients that absolutely kills revenue potential. There is no sales magic wand for closing revenue, but to generate revenue, you need to arm yourself with a carefully considered plan and roll up your sleeves to get things done. All of these pieces work together to achieve financial growth, and how they all play together characterizes the revenue game.

Closing Isn't Selling

Up to this point, I have been downplaying the ability to "sell"; I even called it a bad word in business. However, the reality is that being a great salesperson is a key piece of the formula. I just wanted you to see the importance of structure and how it plays a major role in the process, because quite often it is overlooked. Knowing how to close business is critical to generating revenue. In *The Tipping Point*, Malcolm Gladwell discusses Salesmen and "their ability to persuade us when we are unconvinced of what we are hearing" (p. 70). I don't know if Mr. Gladwell has ever closed a deal in his life, but he absolutely nails it in this sentence. You see, closing isn't about selling people something that they don't need and making them believe they need it. It's not about high pressure and having people crack into the purchase, and it's certainly not about being so annoying that customers say yes just to get you to go away.

Once we created the golf tournament concept, it was a layup to close; even a novice closer would have brought that deal home. But—

and it's a BIG *but*—would an unskilled salesperson have been able to identify the best way to lead that conversation to the close? Closing a pitch doesn't begin with presenting the idea created; it begins with listening to identify what needs to be presented. "The hunters," whose job it is to bring home the meat, do not shoot arrows into the air, hoping that one of them will strike and kill. That's not skill. Disciplined hunters track and listen.

Cold Calling

Now, every salesperson reading this is thinking to himself, "Yeah, I'm a great listener, and I do absolutely exactly what you are writing, Lou." Once again, I'm saying there's no *way* that's true. The majority of salespeople lack the discipline to put in the time necessary to operate in this way, and the average salesperson is focused on selling inventory instead of providing solutions to her potential customer. I can't tell you how many people reach out to me, telling me what I need in order to support my business. Far more often than I should, I get cookie-cutter proposals in e-mails in which the salesperson states that he has just "created this package for TrinityOne."

Allow me to translate: "I ripped your logo off your Web site and put it on a package, so it's customized."

When people get that kind of e-mail, this is what they think: "*Loser.* This person has no interest in my business and its success. All she cares about is coercing me to pay money for things that will never help me in any way."

If you are operating this way, get out of sales; you're the person who's giving sales a bad name. How is it possible that a salesperson who has never met me and has no idea what my strategy is can provide me with solutions that will propel my organization? *How is this possible?* It's possible only if the salesperson is a magician. Guess what: I don't believe in magic. Magic is sleight of hand and misdirection, just like that sales approach. How many of you have seen initiatives that companies are executing, and you scratch your head and say, "What the heck were they thinking?" I promise you, you're seeing the effects of proposals that were "sold in" and not created specifically to achieve goals.

Just last week, I got a proposal from a company asking us to be a presenting sponsor of a golf tournament. The cost to sponsor the one-day event was $50,000, and, as the person who sent it to me stated, "That will even get you a second foursome." Wow, where do I sign?

First of all, TrinityOne is a small boutique marketing strategy consultancy. We are not IMG. But even if we were, how would the joker who sent this proposal even know whether it made sense for us? I had never chatted with him about our goals, direction, or needs. In fact, *I had never met him*. This was his first encounter with me. This big opportunity to play golf for $50,000 was in a cold-call e-mail. That dude should be fired. While I have half a mind to call him out, I'm sure he will self-destruct without any help from me.

Do you see the lunacy here? The best way to lose potential business is to send me a blind proposal selling me dormant inventory. I'm not a fan of the cold call in general, but I understand that it is a necessary evil in the new business game. If you have to engage in a cold call, don't be foolish. Go about it this way:

> Hi Malcolm,
>
> During the process of building a sports complex like the one your group is developing, much of the expertise is provided by the architects and builders. While they provide insight and experience in infrastructure, program, and safety, they are not always experienced with the day-to-day business of using the stadium to generate revenue after it is built. This makes absolute sense; that's not their function. However, they still make recommendations about signage configuration and other elements that affect revenue-generating opportunities. In order to optimize the results of those recommendations, the design team should always be connected with the marketing and sales group from the get-go so changes can be made without incurring additional design fees.
>
> When I was the chief marketing officer of the New England Patriots and Gillette Stadium and the COO of the New England Revolution, ownership involved my team and me in the plan-

ning, and we were able to help optimize the design and direction to make sure we could maximize revenue generation once the building was complete. It makes so much sense, given the dollars that are being invested in a sports complex, to tap into proven expertise to ensure that the architects and builders can have a real understanding of what's necessary for revenue generation. If those ideas aren't communicated effectively, the effect on revenue can be enormous. The cost of incorporating marketing expertise into the planning is a slight fraction of the expenses you'll save and the revenue you will generate.

I am not positive that we are the right fit for you, but I would be interested in setting up some time to further explore how we could aid your efforts. All indications from our research point to a group like ours being an asset to your project. We are ready to get on a plane and make the investment of time, resources, and money in finding out more because we are confident in our abilities and proven track record.

If you do not have any objection, I will put a call in to you later this week to discuss the possibility of us meeting, or, if you prefer, we can schedule a time to chat on the phone. Please let me know either way.

My best,

Lou

Lou Imbriano
President & CEO
TrinityOne Worldwide

This introductory letter is an absolute cold call for new business. Well, I guess it's a cold letter, because I do not think it's wise or appropriate to just pick up the phone and call someone you have never met or been introduced to. The letter is the beginning of forming a relationship (rather than making a pitch) because it possesses the three Rs for all initial cold-call interactions: (1) research, (2) respect, and (3) record. If you're fortunate enough to have the fourth R, referral, it takes the cold out of the call and makes it lukewarm. Those three Rs are the factors that result in a meeting, which is the only purpose of a cold call. Start with the three Rs:

★ **Research.** Do your homework and make sure there is a true purpose for a meeting, not just one that you assume. Understand facts about the company, and get a feel for what it is all about. Never tell the person how to do his business. Always include words like, "It appears to me," or, "I believe we could be a fit." Show the recipient of the letter that you did some work prior to sending a letter.

★ **Respect.** Show the person to whom you are writing that you understand that she is busy and you do not want to be an intrusion, but that you have taken the steps necessary to make certain that you will not waste her time. You might not be the right fit, but your reason for meeting is thoughtful and has merit.

★ **Record.** Your track record of performance is definitely pertinent. Give the prospect a glimpse of what you are all about so he knows that you can back up what you or your company is all about. This will give him comfort and win you respect in return.

If you include these three elements in an introductory letter, it will make it much harder for the recipient to avoid you. Sure, it can and will happen, but the Rs are really three reasons for the recipient to think twice about discarding you. If the recipient ignores you, you have stated that you will reach out to her, and that's where, if you are considerate and show persistence, you will eventually create an opportunity to meet. If you have the luxury of the fourth R, the referral, your success rate should be dancing at the 90 percent level.

★ **Referral.** If you can include in the letter that a colleague or friend of the recipient made the recommendation that you reach out, you dramatically multiply the chances of a successful letter. Always follow the lead of the person who referred you. The call or letter should always begin, "Joe Limone suggested that I should reach out to you" (and, of course, use the name of the person who actually referred you).

Please, never, ever, ever send a letter that starts, "To whom this may concern." Don't laugh: I got one today. Do you think I responded? Always remember that the process is one of carefully placing building blocks that get you to the next level. The cold call is the first block to get you to the next meeting.

When you go out on a first date, do you get on one knee and ask the woman you just met for her hand in marriage? Of course not; she'd think you were a complete psycho. When legitimate businesspeople get proposals on the first interaction, they think you are just as nuts. Now, not only have you shanked the first impression, but the likelihood is also that you are not getting a mulligan. Why would you operate in a way that sets you up for only one shot at a yes? That's what salespeople are setting themselves up for when they sell rather than build a sale.

If you're the person at your company who is responsible for closing business, you probably view yourself as the "hunter" we talked about in previous chapters. We use the word *hunter* to point out that it's the salespeople who go out and get the money in the same way that hunters go out and kill the food. While the term *hunter* is great for a job description, it's terrible for explaining *how* the job is done. We joke about how in caveman days, you'd club someone over the head and drag her back to your cave if you wanted to partner with her—in today's society, if you club someone over the head, you go to jail. Hunters, as single-minded as they may be, still have to build relationships. As a salesperson, you are not going out for the kill. Remember: you're implementing the new ABCs of selling, and you're *creating*.

From today forward, you are a new business executive. You are building new business, and you're an extension of your company's marketing department. Why? Thinking of yourself as an extension of marketing, whether the official company structure supports that or not, will help you not only find opportunities for your brand to separate itself from your competitors, but also engage and interact with your consumers.

These are pretty simple ideas, yet organizations quite often do not properly engage with new business potential because the people who are selling lose sight of their connection to marketing and their real objective: helping people create new business opportunities and assisting them as they build relationships with their current customers.

Don't get caught up in the sins of slick marketers or forceful salespeople; you have to avoid the Seven Deadly Sins of Sales and Marketing. In addition to the good habits that we are trying to help build upon, we also need to assist you in avoiding the pitfalls.

SEVEN DEADLY SINS OF SALES AND MARKETING

We're bring back the Catholic school references again, this time with the Seven Deadly Sins of Sales and Marketing. Let's face it: salespeople often have a bad rap, and the truth is because it's often warranted. If you want to be a salesperson who's closing business, building great relationships, and is never mistaken for someone slinging snake oil, you absolutely must avoid these seven major pitfalls.

Greed

When the sale is viewed as a transactional deal rather than an arrangement designed to build relationships with customers, this is a sign of greed. Greed creeps in when sales forces care only about their sales revenue goals and gouge the clients and consumers with high-priced one-off deals that have no chance for success. A great example of this happened to me the other day. I was driving to the ballpark with my dad and my kids, and the closer I got to Fenway, the higher the prices went up for parking. Just outside the stadium, the parking fee was $60. Typically, that lot charged $20. It was seizing on a supply and demand situation, and it couldn't have cared less about its customers. It was all about the revenue per vehicle, and it could do this because people didn't have any other option. That may work in that situation, but by no means should it be the way you operate in selling your goods or services.

Gluttony

You know you're dealing with gluttony when the quantity of deals is more important than the quality, and the salesperson has no desire to service the relationship to the level that she should. She has no desire to make sure the product suits the customer or that the type of service accomplishes the needs of the customer. The goal is based purely on numbers and not on depth of experience for the client. This reminds me of the stereotypical used car salesman who couldn't care less if the vehicle is a lemon; his job is to get cars off the lot. It's become a common sales caricature: the guy who will say anything in order to move inventory. When you are creating a relationship in order to close revenue, you have to be straight and not spin, even a little, to get the sale.

Envy

Envy boils up when other new business executives close business and competitive organizations out-work, out-hustle, and out-close you and your organization. You cannot get caught up in the success of others to the point that it deters or prevents you from achieving your goals. Envy ultimately takes your eye off the ball and makes you lose focus on what needs to be accomplished. Stop, appreciate others' success for a minute or two, and then get off your butt and work harder to get the job done.

Sloth

When a company or individual lets closed business and relationships lie dormant after the contract is signed, it's fallen into sloth. I've said this again and again, but closing a deal is not the end of the sale; it's just the beginning. Now that you have brought the relationship into the organization, you have a customer who is partial to your products and services. This is when great sales and marketing executives turn the new business into organic growth. New business needs to be catered to the extreme and treated as a growth opportunity rather than as money in the bank. Here's where your group needs to learn more about the particular consumer and capitalize on what you learn.

Pride

Sales and Marketing cannot fall into the trap of pride and become consumed with having created great initiatives and driven revenues—this type of pride leads to resting on one's laurels. Marketing is like the Earth: round and continuously moving. It's not flat, with a beginning and an end. A company's marketing tactics and the way it treats its consumers have to be evolving constantly. Making statements like, "We're number one," or, "The best in the field," is a clear indicator of an impending fall from glory. IBM was untouchable at one point—the biggest and the best—and its fall was very far and highly publicized. *MIT Sloan Management Review* points to IBM's failure in a July 1996 piece. In the late 1980s and early 1990s, IBM was viewed by many as "a dinosaur, an implosion—a wreck" because of its operations decisions and failure to remake itself fast enough to meet consumers' technology needs. This ultimately led to a 1993 reorganization: in 1993 the *New York Times* wrote that IBM reported losses of $40 million and had to lay off 35,000 employees and send 25,000 into early retirement. Microsoft's approach allowed it to take the lead in the industry; IBM was left at a standstill and it wasn't until new management came in and changed its direction that IBM saw any sort of resurgence. Every time one of the greats falls, it's because its pride in what it has accomplished and the arrogance of its leadership prevent change and operating in the now.

Lust

When a salesperson becomes totally obsessed with and continually lusts after closing one perfect deal, it's easy to abandon business sense and make poor decisions. Forethought about potential negative consequences goes out the window when someone becomes so consumed with the ultimate close; small deals end up being pushed to the wayside. We fell into that trap at TrinityOne early on, when we were representing Richard Childress Racing. We received a percentage of all the sales we brought in, so we got caught up in selling the hood of the car. The price of that particular sponsorship is around $20 to $25 million annually—which represents a very hefty seven-figure commission. Because of the time we spent on the big score, we didn't work as much as we should have on smaller deals, and, quite frankly, we might have been able to get a few more singles and doubles if we hadn't been just swinging for the fence. We got sucked into the excitement of the big close. It was a mistake and a misuse of efforts.

Wrath

When frustration between Sales and Marketing mounts and they're not working together to accomplish company goals as opposed to individual department agendas, they incur the wrath of each other and of the owners. This is typically more common when Sales and Marketing are in their own silos and not under one umbrella: the energy they burn one-upping each other to gain favor over the other regardless of their real results or company goals is counterproductive.

Sales and Marketing have a love-hate sibling rivalry in most situations, which is amplified when they are separated within an organization. This is most easily managed when one leader manages the two groups as a single entity; having the two groups fall under a single leader yields the best results. We witnessed this at the Patriots: when we were structured as one group, we were ultimately far more productive.

Sales and Marketing can be an unbelievable engine for an organization, but only when they're utilizing an all-encompassing strategy that ensures that they are working together toward a common goal that complements both groups' efforts. This carefully orchestrated complementary behavior catapults revenue growth into the stratosphere.

Building, not selling, requires an organization to consider sales, marketing, relationship architecture, operations, and customer service as spokes in a wheel that propels business.

Now that we have that business wheel ready to roll, we're going to talk through the steps needed to fuel it. Once a new business team is equipped with the tools to build, it can take the necessary steps to ensure that it generates revenue for the organization. Of course, relationships equal revenue only if you know how to capitalize on and convert them, so let's talk about how to go make some money.

REVENUE GENERATION: THE NEW BUSINESS FUNNEL

At this point, it should come as no surprise when I tell you that the key to new business development is, at its root, being an extremely disciplined salesperson, both in your personal organization/operation and in the steps you take to close business. Most salespeople are so wound up about closing business and making money that they're not inclined to perform patiently and thoughtfully. They are always thinking about getting deals *done*—and often—so it's natural that they rush clients to the close.

Great salespeople, however, have "game" and know how to utilize the *process* of selling to achieve their ultimate goal. When they spend time with clients and potential customers, they know that closing the business is the white elephant in the room, but they never talk about it, refer to it, or even so much as allude to wanting money from the potential client. They follow the rules of engagement until a particular, precise moment, and then—and only then—they attempt to close business. They know that each step in the process has to be taken, and they understand that it's impossible to rush or skip any of the steps if they want reliable results. The cultivated ability to take their time, to masterfully hit all the key elements of closing business, is what gives them game.

Experience and simply knowing the steps, in and of themselves, are not what develop game; confidence that taking these steps will lead to revenue also plays a major role. There are many different sales techniques and strategies for closing business, but I'm not going to get into "sales training." This is not about selling; it's about building and, as with anything you set out to build, you need to follow a blueprint. Just as we've talked about designing your business-to-consumer revenue generation, now we'll turn to business-to-business situations and explore the nine elements we believe are crucial for leading you to new business and generating revenue for your organization.

THE NINE STEPS OF THE NEW BUSINESS FUNNEL

1. Prospecting
2. Research
3. Identify your target list (short list)
4. Relationship Architecture
5. Needs analysis
6. Create a pertinent program
7. Pitch the concept
8. Exchange ideas to get to the close
9. Close/dead

1. Prospecting

It's important to go into new business development mindful that your organization has a particular makeup and set of characteristics that make it unique. Like any company, it has articulated goals and chooses to operate in a specific fashion. As you're thinking about potential prospects, think beyond your products and services, which obviously have to be correlated, and begin to look for other organizations whose business practices and consumer bases are related to your own. I'm asking you to thoughtfully consider how your group is a match with other companies in culture, direction, and purpose; these connections will lead you to your long list of prospects. As you begin to assess the potential of a particular company, take the time to list the areas of commonality between the company you are sizing up and your own. Here are the areas you should typically focus on:

★ **Target demographics.** Ensure that you're both trying to reach the same kinds of people.

★ **Brand quality and positioning.** If you're offering luxury products, be discerning about whom you approach that you'd like to associate with your brand.

★ **Types of programs that you currently execute.** If you're already running similar promotions and loyalty programs, it'll be easier to find ways to complement each other.

★ **Brands that you already associate with.** You may find it easier to show compatibility if you're already working with the same brands.

In fact, you should always keep these characteristics in mind when you prospect for new clients; they're a great mechanism for sorting through the sea of potential customers out there and matching a new company with your brand. For example, if you're a Web designer or a social media strategist, make sure that your past experience and clients align with the potential targets you're identifying. Those similarities are what resonate most with new clients.

Nevertheless, and most important, never try to force the relationship. Even if you're convinced that the match is perfect, you still need to let the relationship develop properly. This is especially important if the connections you're drawing are a bit far-fetched. If you're already great at what you do, thinking this way will help you find many opportunities that reflexively fit. Begin with the obvious connections, and don't spend your energy on ones that seem like a stretch. Your diligence in this area will save you time and effort as you move closer to the close. Once you begin seriously pursuing a client after your prospecting stage, the amount of work you'll do to get to revenue is significant. Don't waste time on prospects that are long shots.

I'm going to oversimplify this for the purpose of making my point. Imagine that you're working for a NASCAR team; connecting with other businesses that sell gas, tires, and oil makes sense. It's a no-brainer to begin there. Meanwhile, Victoria's Secret may be a stretch, so put that off to the side for now. I'm *not* saying that Victoria's Secret holds zero potential for the future, but why begin there? Similarly, if you're Barilla Pasta, you'll be looking to connect with restaurants, supermarkets, and hotels.

This sounds ridiculously obvious, but you would be shocked at what I've heard salespeople offer as realistic paths to revenue. I once worked with a guy in radio who, if you asked him what company would fit with Barilla Pasta, would say, "The Christmas Tree Shop," because people use pasta for arts and crafts projects. I admire the creativity, but you do not want your new business people focusing on this type of long shot.

At the Patriots, one of my sales reps once wanted to add Entenmann's Bakery to his list. This was a difficult one to determine because, while signage and promotion were probably too costly and not a right fit, its sales team did some entertaining. We agreed that it might be worth a try to see if we could create a hospitality program that might work for Entenmann's; perhaps we could develop a great way for the company to entertain using the Patriots brand. Given that we already had a deal with Stop and Shop, we thought maybe there was a vendor co-op possibility with our tailgating promotion. My gut still told me it was a stretch, but the list-to-list comparison showed potential.

These cases are tough, because they're not as far-fetched as Barilla Pasta at The Christmast Tree Shop. In situations like the one with Entenmann's, despite the doubt, we put them on the list because, frankly, generating revenue was our job. Unfortunately, when you put a long shot on the long list because of a mere glimmer of hope, it tends to migrate to the short list. You have to understand that the amount of time you spend on a potential client that *doesn't* show revenue is typically *just as much* as the amount of time that goes into one that *does*. That's why being selective is so important. Don't get me wrong; if you do things right, you're still building a relationship, and that can always be useful in the long term. But when you are trying to reach individual sales goals, you want to make sure your short list is solid.

In the case of Entenmann's Bakery, it turned out that my instincts were right and we weren't able to close it, but at least there was a legitimate rationale behind the decision to pursue it. At times I feel that sales folks just see another company spending money *anywhere* and, simply by virtue of that company's ability to spend, it hits the target list for business. This kind of impulsive move is devoid of the discipline of prospecting that's integral to consistently closing business.

Remember, you're going to close only a percentage of the prospects in the new business funnel, and the particular percentage will vary depending on your industry. If you're doing it right, though, that percentage should become fairly consistent and predictable. That's why it is crucial that you select legitimate prospects; you do not want to disguise your funnel with false hope. If your goal is five new deals and it typically takes one hundred prospects to get you to that number, you need to know that. Padding your funnel with long shots only skews your results to a lower close rate and wastes your time. It's imperative that you be honest and avoid stretching reality as you identify prospects. This honesty will ultimately raise your close rate.

Once you have a solid long list, you can't just rush out and cold-call them. Your research isn't done yet; you need to go deeper still in order to make certain that the prospect is actually worth your time and effort. Your time is money. Do not squander it. Do your homework, and find a connection that can turn your long list into an initial target list. At the Patriots, we decided that 50 to 75 was a manageable number of prospects for each sales rep. Your short list has to be long enough to get you to your sales goals, yet short enough that it's manageable, because you'll need to be able to work on all the prospects on that list at the same time. To get to that short list, you must do some research. This will either validate your long list or weed out targets that appeared to hold potential, but really do not.

2. Research

Developing the long list of prospects isn't the end of your prospecting, and having a long list of potential prospects doesn't mean that you'll automatically call on each of them. You'll be using this list to dig more deeply and collect information about each of the companies and the attributes that link your brand to that company and the individuals who work there. Whether you have a huge staff and three assistants or you're running the show single-handedly, you can't make excuses: the intel you gather about a company and its goods and services can't be superficial. You have to invest significant *time* in learning significant *information* about the organization that you intend to pitch. The good news is that if you are real during the process, you will be able to easily classify the low-hanging fruit on the list and winnow them out from the long shots that made it onto your original long list.

At the Patriots, and now at TrinityOne, the members of the marketing staff work with new business executives to retrieve as much pertinent information as possible about the prospect and develop that prospect's profile in our company profile system; the system was specifically designed to gather and store in-depth information. When creating a profile, you want to include information on both the company in general and the important executives and staff members within the company. Let's look at all the avenues you can use to create these profiles, first to assist you in determining whom it makes sense to pursue, and second as an ongoing reference guide to that particular company:

★ **Company Web site.** Because we're living in the age of transparency, you may be pleasantly surprised at some of the information you can find here, both about the corporation and about the individuals within it. If a company is public, you can even find information like annual reports, earnings, leadership, and board members. A company's news or press page often includes recent announcements, media coverage, and important changes going on inside the company.

★ **Social media.** Researchers everywhere should be thankful for social media, which provides a different, more dynamic look into companies and executives. Check Twitter and Facebook for corporate pages. Corporate pages will give you insight into exciting promotions, partnerships, product launches, store openings, and the overall tone and personality of the company. You should also be able to gauge its level of customer service from the way it communicates with consumers who interact with it. Look into LinkedIn pages for individuals as well. Again, you might very well be amazed at the type and depth of information people share on these sites. You may be able to find information like employment history, education, family (marital status/kids), vacation history, books they've read, and music they enjoy. An incredible depth of knowledge can be gained from even the quickest search of social media.

★ **Blogs.** Blogs are another great tool for understanding the personality of a company and its brand message. Some companies enlist specific staff members to maintain their corporate blogs; other times, you may get lucky enough to find a staff member's personal blog. Both are great for compiling information for profiles and allowing you to really understand a company's philosophy and positioning. There are also nuances on the personalities of the individuals who are posting. Blogs are the sliding glass doors to the soul of a company and can bear a great deal of fruitful information.

★ **Search engines.** Instead of paying for expensive news services and research tools, you have a wealth of information at your fingertips with the Internet and major search engines like Google and Bing. Conduct a news search on the company you are profiling, and do a search on each of the key executives and contacts you'd be meeting with. Search as you begin the profile, but then continue to search on an ongoing basis to keep up to date on important information as it becomes available.

You can even set up a Google Alert that delivers relevant, timely news stories to your inbox via e-mail. How easy is that? If and when you schedule a meeting with this company, you or your staff should check for recent news up until that meeting. If you have a meeting at 3 p.m., and the company announces at 10 a.m. that it has bought another company, you should know that before walking into your meeting.

Corporate executives are often "out and about" in the community, serving on boards, speaking at events and seminars, and being profiled or quoted in articles. You are likely to find all this type of information through a basic search. In your search, you may even uncover political contributions, which give you a little more information to work with.

★ **People.** Talk to people who know the company and its employees. Let's face it: it's a small world, and you may already know someone who is working there or affiliated with it—even someone who knows someone who is married to someone else's cousin. Great information comes from all sources, and the more information you can gather from the inside, the better. When you or your staff is working to book a meeting, you're often talking with an assistant, and you should always be listening to the type of unsolicited information you get in these situations. Just remember that hearsay should be treated as "unconfirmed" and noted as such in a profile.

★ **Work in progress.** Profiles should never be finished and always be evolving; consider them and treat them as perpetual works in progress. After a meeting with a particular company occurs, there should always be a debriefing with those in attendance to find out even more information on the company. While the meeting itself should solicit a wealth of information to add to the company profile, sitting in a lobby or reception area prior to the meeting often provides some very intriguing information about the company and its executives. You never know what a chatty receptionist or assistant may be talking about, so always keep your ears open.

EXTRA POINTS
To view a sample profile format, please log onto
http://louimbriano.com/winningthecustomer-reference.

Don't lose sight of the objective here. You're working to acquire as much info as possible for two reasons: if you have done your job, you will absolutely know, (1), whether the company fits with your goods and services, and (2), how to speak intelligently about and with the company with which you are hoping to form a partnership. If you have a legitimate hypothesis about why this company fits with your group, you'll find it much easier to persuade the company that you can help its business.

I realize this appears to be a lot of work, but this is the part that will make the rest of your efforts precise, efficient, and more effective. However, you need to keep in mind that the profile you create in this step is just the foundation for the comprehensive analysis of a company that you'll continually update. Every interaction will allow new information to aid you in your efforts.

3. Identify Your Target List (Short List)

Your long list is made up of 50 to 75 companies that you believe fit with your organization's goods and services. After your initial research is complete and you get a better feel for which will be the right fit for your company, certain companies will float to the top. These 10 to 15 companies will leap off the page, practically screaming, "We make sense!"

Begin with this list—which is *not* to say, "And forget the remaining 50." We'll get back to them in a bit. Again: because the new business process can be lengthy, particularly depending on the industry you are in, you should be addressing every position in the new business funnel at all times. If you are going to be successful in new business development, it isn't going to be because you picked out 10 companies, followed the steps, and then closed them. Relying on these top 10 and ditching the rest is a sure way to fail. You must have potential clients at every level of the funnel.

Your ultimate responsibility and objective is to constantly have a business flow that helps you close business on a regular basis and not sporadically. Even if you view new business strategically, you're still dealing with a numbers game. The more legitimately realistic targets you have at different levels of the funnel, the better positioned you are to continually close new business. You can call on 500 companies and close 2 deals, or you can focus strategically on 75 companies and close 7. If you'd rather do the latter, the new business funnel will allow you to be more precise in your efforts.

Once you narrow down your short list, expend a larger percentage of your focus and efforts on this group: after all, they are the low-hanging fruit. Your job is to move them through the funnel and close business. There will be another time to climb higher up and out onto a limb that also bears fruit—it's more work, so get the easier stuff first.

Successfully identifying the company you should be working with is only half the battle; now you need to identify specifically whom you should begin building a relationship with to ultimately achieve your desired results. It could be a very obvious person, such as the one who actually makes the expenditure decisions, or it could be another person in the group that actually assists in the decision-making process. Maybe you decide you need to target multiple people. Either way, it is at this stage that you must begin sorting that out. Because business relationships tend to be more fluid, you probably will make adjustments to the funnel on an ongoing basis to determine what individual(s) will lead you to close.

Don't make the mistake that so many sales professionals who think they're skilled and experienced tend to make and jump into cold calling—it's a misstep that can cost real money. Jumping in simply lowers their close ratio. Don't skip these crucial relationship-building steps.

4. Relationship Architecture

We have discussed what it means to be a Relationship Architect at great length, but now it's time to put it into practice to make money for your company and yourself. Now that you have an idea about who it is that you should be working with and preliminary details about his organization, you have to invest more time and dig even deeper to fully understand the company and your main contacts. Keep in mind that up until this point, *you have not even approached the company you ultimately hope to close.*

Your purpose at this stage is twofold: to learn as much as you can about the company and its makeup, and to do the same with the individual contacts. The difference between this stage and the research step is that now you will be gathering intel directly from individuals within the company while building solid relationships with its key employees. Relationship building should be your main focus. Work to set up a face-to-face meeting in the office or another opportunity to get together that's appropriate and will help you build trust and credibility.

The objective here is to use this meeting as a relationship accelerant. These sorts of events and invitations differ from memorable moments in that your goal is to get information *from* your potential clients rather than to create memories *for* them. People love to get out of the office, and bringing them into a less formal atmosphere can bring their guard down and free them up to communicate more openly. This is a great way to speed up your ability to find out who these people are and what they're all about.

I met Jack Shields from Shields MRI when I was at the Patriots. Jack was a big Patriots fans and saw the benefit of working with the team to help support the Shields MRI brand and to help his group build relationships. Shields turned into a tremendous partner of the team, and we worked on the relationship constantly to grow it and make it stronger.

I believe we accomplished that to the fullest and created a true win-win situation. When I left the team, Jack was one of the first calls I made to tell him about my new company, TrinityOne. Because Shields MRI spent money in sports marketing and that was our specialty, I had short-listed it as a group that I believed we could assist with its efforts.

I already had a very strong bond with Jack and great relationships with others in his organization. I also spent time with Jack's dad, Tom Sr., his brother Tommy, and their top marketing executive, John Antaya. I built relationships throughout the organization to support the one I had with Jack. Let's make this clear: my relationship with the organization was *not* just with the marketing executive. Moreover, I didn't just end my relationship building with Jack: he was the president and made the decisions about spending, but one relationship in a company is only the beginning. Jack and I chatted often, we golfed, and we went out to eat. I took him out on our boat—the whole nine yards. Every activity was designed to help build the relationship and understand better how, now at TrinityOne, we could assist Shields MRI in doing business. Don't get me wrong; by this time, my relationship with Jack had grown beyond business. We were friends, and it's not as if Jack didn't know I wanted his business.

Even though I had built a great relationship with Jack and Shields MRI, TrinityOne had been up and running for two years, and we didn't have a business relationship with Shields MRI. This should have been the low-hanging fruit we discussed earlier. It wasn't until I took Jack to a Boston Celtics game and we sat on the floor that things began to germinate—from floor seats, just like the ones Jack Nicholson sits in when he goes to Los Angeles Lakers games. Jack Shields had been to plenty of Celtics games, but until that point, he had never sat on the parquet. The perspective opened up the conversation about working with the Celtics and having TrinityOne assist in the negotiations and execution of Shields MRI's sports marketing initiatives. The conversation led to a follow-up meeting and eventually a contract, which led to TrinityOne's becoming Shields MRI's sports marketing agency of record. It took two years and consistent work on a prospect in the new business funnel *with whom I already had a relationship* to close business.

The time invested in the relationship is crucial, but the unique setting was the trigger for actually doing business. That discussion was key, and it might not have occurred if the event hadn't fit perfectly with our goals. It was an accelerant for doing business, even though I had committed two years to figuring out how TrinityOne fit with Shields MRI. Perhaps if I'd invited Jack to floor seats just after I left the Patriots, we would have done business sooner.

Accelerants are great, but the important thing to note during the Relationship Architecture step of the new business funnel is that while you are meeting and investing time, be sure to record as much knowledge as possible about the individual and the company in the profile. That will ultimately be the road map that will lead you to closing business.

Let's talk about a tough lesson we learned about building relationships inside companies. Although I had very good relationships with Tom Sr., Tommy, and John, I really invested most of my time with Jack. That relationship was the glue to our business. I worked with Tommy and John on a few things, especially the Bruins deal that we negotiated for Shields MRI, but I obviously built the relationship in such a way that I was "Jack's guy." I thought I was doing all the right things, and never in a million years would I have thought Jack would step down as president of the company. But lo and behold, nothing in life is certain, and Jack decided he was going to break off and start his own group. As Homer Simpson would say, "D'oh." You know what's coming—when the economy began to turn and budgets got tight, our contract with Shields MRI was not renewed.

I know we had done a great job for them. I know Tommy and John were pleased with our performance; they expressed that often. Perhaps if I had spent more time on those relationships, it would have been harder for them to not renew. Learn from my mistake: you never know when your primary contact and relationship will move on or be removed. Make sure you build relationships deep into the organization and not just with one individual. I typically do that, and I believe I did so at Shields as well, but I let the fact that Jack's last name was Shields lull me into a false sense of security. I just had coffee with Tommy the other day, but I think I took it for granted that Jack would be there forever and probably did not fully solidify the other organizational relationships as much as I could have. Don't fall victim to that potential pitfall like I did.

Building a strong relationship with individuals throughout an organization is a major part of closing new business. At some point, your efforts *cannot* be about the individual, and you have to keep in mind the company's goals and what it needs to achieve them. If you take into consideration only the individual relationship and neglect the company's business needs, you will fall short and may ultimately lose your relationship with the company.

5. Needs Analysis

Comprehensive needs analysis is what will prevent you from falling into the pitfall of relying too heavily on the relationship. It's imperative that, while building a relationship with individuals within a company, you also gain an understanding of the company's specific goals and needs. It takes real effort to know what another company wants to achieve and think about how your company can assist in the process. It's important to understand how the company wants to stand out in the crowd and communicate with its consumer. You're going to create a needs analysis sheet for every short-listed prospect. You won't be basing its content on your assumptions or your research, but on thoughtful questioning of not only your primary contact, but also others within the organization that you are trying to do business with. This makes it even more important that your relationships permeate throughout the company. The more comfortable its employees are with you, the more forthcoming they will be with the information you need to know for the next phase in acquiring the company's business.

Some of this can be done informally, but I always find that you still need to have a few meetings in which you come right out and tell the people at the company that in order to know whether you can assist them, you need to know more about their objectives in detail. Go into a meeting being very up front about your intention to ask a million questions in the hopes of helping them. During the session, the individuals at the company should give you a clear picture of their efforts and even where they have fallen short—and *this* is where you will find out if and how you can help. Never will your prior relationship building be more important, because if you were to lead with something like this, it could be counterproductive. This meeting is not the initial fact-finding meeting where you are listening (although at times you will get lucky and people will talk to you early on and divulge crucial information). This kind of exchange happens most frequently when you have built trust and it is clear to the individuals you have been working with that your company could potentially be a solution for them.

This meeting does *not* come out of a cold call.

I got caught in this trap with Boston Beer years back. The salesperson who was assigned to Boston Beer—the company that produces Sam Adams beer—indicated to me that he needed my assistance in a needs analysis meeting that he expected would lead us to a presentation on one of our properties. The meeting began, and I, naturally, started asking some pretty detailed questions; it seemed odd to me, but the person we were meeting with was clearly uncomfortable with sharing all the information. Now, I had understood that the sales rep had done the proper prep work and relationship building prior to this meeting, but I found out that this was the absolute first in-person meeting anyone from our organization had ever had with that gentleman. It was very awkward and uncomfortable because at one point in the meeting, this guy expressed just how completely confused he was about why we were asking such detailed questions. He was probably even more alarmed by our approach because most people expect the transactional approach and are totally unaccustomed to anyone asking these kinds of questions.

The prospect felt as if total strangers were grilling him because my sales executive felt that it was acceptable to leapfrog steps. Needless to say, this effort resulted in complete failure. Sure, you can get lucky at times, but there is enormous risk in doing so, and this book isn't about the one lucky moment. It doesn't matter if someone really *should* work with you or you're a great business match: once you make someone feel uncomfortable, you can rest assured you'll never get another meeting or opportunity to build the relationship.

Let's pause here for a second and reiterate: even if you are asking the right questions that should theoretically get you to the right outcome, if you introduce this part of the process prematurely, you risk the building of a relationship and doing business with that individual. Remember, we started this chapter by noting that a disciplined approach is fundamentally necessary to closing business. You cannot lose sight of that sense of discipline and process. Yes, people you are working with as potential clients could, and I stress *could*, come around more quickly and see that you could assist their efforts much faster than others in the funnel, but you can *never* assume that this will be the case. Have I skipped steps because I felt I had comfort from the individual to do so? Yes. What typically was the outcome? More often than not, the outcome was failure on one level or another. Do not cut corners with the process, regardless of your gut feeling of things.

There's a great illustration of this in the Kevin Costner movie *Tin Cup*, which is your basic movie about a guy with unfulfilled golf potential who gets a second chance. Whether you loved the movie or not, if you've seen it, you'll admit that it's painful to watch what Costner's character goes through as he is leading the pack at a PGA event, and, instead of taking the strategic approach to win the tournament, he goes for it all in one shot and fails. Then, because he's so convinced he can make the shot, he repeats the *same* shot over and over again, removing him from any chance of victory. The win was within his grasp, but he tried to shortcut the process—and failed. Stick to the process. Although it may take slightly longer and be more work, it will put you in a position to win every time, not by accident or chance, but through a disciplined process.

When you avoid the process, you're really cheating yourself out of closing business. Each step brings you closer to the prize. Needless to say, we were never able to get another meeting with the person we met with at Boston Beer. He never got what we were trying to accomplish because we skipped steps in the process.

The opposite was true as we walked through the sales process with Fidelity, and it's because TrinityOne's sales executive Andrea Solomita was patient enough to take the essential steps to create the relationship. It was so rewarding to have done the work correctly and to build a program that we knew could assist Fidelity in its efforts to market its 529 college plans. The work resonated, and it led us to additional business and brought TrinityOne an additional new client, the Mass Educational Financial Authority (MEFA). The process took her a bit longer than most people would have the patience to withstand, but Andrea was disciplined, and it paid off.

6. Create a Pertinent Program

Andrea followed the new business funnel and created a relationship with Joe Ciccariello, the vice president of college products at Fidelity. Fidelity was hoping to expand its reach and connect with potential consumers for the 529 college savings program it runs in conjunction with MEFA. Andrea performed an initial needs analysis, and we met with Joe's team for a follow-up to dig a bit deeper into the firm's goals.

Andrea presented all the details she had collected through the needs analysis and incorporated my thoughts to offer an amazing program for Fidelity, despite its somewhat limited budget.

I will say here that we had a bit of an edge because Fidelity had been a client of ours when I was at the Patriots. I knew the organization more intimately than most companies. We met with the Fidelity team on a regular basis to help it with its Patriots, Revolution, and Gillette Stadium initiatives. That being said, we had not previously worked with Joe's team. After getting all the details from Joe's group and understanding the budgetary restrictions, we knew almost instantaneously the right direction to take to assist the group's efforts. The 529 group was, as you would imagine, focused on new acquisitions of families in the 529 program, as well as encouraging families that were already enrolled to invest additional funds into their children's 529 program. It wanted a mechanism to engage both groups. The nature of what Joe's team was looking to accomplish caused two areas to continually surface in our brainstorming sessions: special access and targeted database marketing.

Our biggest hurdle was that the group was funding other large-scale programs, and this was all going to be an add-on project with limited funding. The program that appeared to make the most sense was one that combined a relationship with the New England Revolution, the Mass Youth Soccer Association (MYSA), and Fidelity. Youth sports would serve as an effective, budget-friendly way to reach Fidelity's target audience.

Since I had negotiated the deal with Fidelity for the naming rights for the Fidelity Investments Clubhouse at Gillette Stadium, I was very familiar with the package and the assets that Fidelity had received from the Revolution as part of the deal. As we developed the plan, Fidelity already owned logo rights, tickets, and a number of other assets, including a free use of the stadium. This inventory came in handy as we created a unique soccer experience that combined the Revolution assets with initiatives that targeted the plush MYSA database of soccer families in Massachusetts. Access to that database and some branding at MYSA events came at a minimal cost, but coupling them with the Revolution assets became a very effective program that was within reach of the company's budget. The results were very favorable, and our efforts caught the attention of MEFA, resulting in discussions with MEFA concerning marketing activities, initiatives, and strategic planning that could serve its needs. We ultimately signed MEFA as a new client.

It's safe to say that these results were brought about by Andrea's hard work and patience in the first five steps of the funnel and our ability to create a pertinent program for Fidelity's 529 efforts. When you are at this sixth step in the new business funnel, all the hard work, research, and relationship building pay off. The groundwork you have laid to this point will give you the tools to create initiatives that fit perfectly with the client. With Fidelity, we were able not only to understand its needs but also to uncover the knowledge that led us to use the Revolution assets as part of the program to assist in accomplishing its goals. If you collect strong information in the process, creating programs that make sense for a potential client in the sixth step is very easy to accomplish.

You also have to be honest with yourself the entire time. If the fit isn't there, or if the solution that you can provide isn't appropriate for the prospect, you cannot force an idea on a potential client. There has to be a logical fit for your company and the prospect. Quite often, sales executives will push an idea that makes little sense just to try to get the sale. Sure, occasionally the prospect will bite, but this goes back to transactional sales and leaves the longevity of your deal and your relationship in the lurch anyway. If you need a hammer to make the concept fit, there's a pretty good chance that it's not the right program or idea, and you won't win the trust of the customer, whether you have his money or not. You'll do much better to be totally up front and say that you are not a good fit at this time and cannot solve his current need. If you approach it this way, even though you forgo short-term gains, you add another layer of credibility. When you come straight out and truthfully say that you can't help, how do you think you will be received the next time when you make the statement that you can help the business achieve its goals? I would have to think the business would be yours purely because of your credibility.

In order to create a pertinent program, you have to listen intently to what the prospect wants and *give* that *to her*. I have met with sales reps in the past who were trying to persuade us to buy into their programs or services. If I explained what our company did, in fact, need in order to grow, these reps would come back with a retrofitted collection of all the inventory they wanted to sell me, repackaged in a way that made it appear that it would help us achieve our goals. That's not what I am talking about here. You need to actually provide solutions and not inventory. If you can't imagine a client for whom you can provide a solution, you need to rethink your own business, not theirs. This is not about prepackaged solutions; it's entirely about customizing solutions for results. The difference is dramatic when it comes to closing and retaining business. This is where, as a new businessperson, you have to get out of the La-Z-Boy and roll up your sleeves to win the customer over. This is also why you are better positioned when you have a team that is made up of marketing operational staff, salespeople, and creative people. The collaboration gets you to the very best solutions your company can offer.

It makes me absolutely crazy when I go to a sporting event, and during the stoppage in action, there is a promotion for a "Seat Upgrade," where two people are taken from seats up in the higher tiers of the stadium and brought into two primo seats. Invariably, that seat upgrade is brought to you by a sponsor, like Pennzoil, Subway, or a hospital. What on *earth* does the concept of a seat upgrade have to do with any of these brands or the industries they are in? This is a clear indicator that a salesperson was selling inventory that she had available, as opposed to creating something that works for the client. Now, if the Seat Upgrade was brought to you by

JetBlue and the copy that went with the promotion was, "With in-seat entertainment and more legroom in every aisle, flying JetBlue is like getting a seat upgrade on any other airline," then the promotion is pertinent to the client, and it's using it as a mechanism to let customers know that flying is more comfortable and enjoyable when they fly JetBlue.

In sports, teams would have a great opportunity to be the Zamboni and take a great chunk of a company's marketing budget off the table if only they stopped looking at the inventory they're still holding and instead looked at what the brand engaging with them needs to accomplish. I realize it's not as simple if you are selling copiers to potential clients, where the units may be exactly the same as those being sold by your competitor, but that's when you and your team become an integral part of the package. You are not just selling a business machine; you have to be part of the solution, whether that means being there at a moment's notice if something goes wrong or providing honest guidance when the client is looking to expand his capabilities. In these cases, you'd better believe you are part of the package.

Whether you are creating this all-encompassing sports marketing program to drive consumers to buy a particular brand's products or you are complementing the products you sell with your expertise to help your client do business, the program you persuade a potential client to purchase has to be pertinent to his needs, not yours.

7. Pitch the Concept

OK, now, and *only* now, it is time to create a proposal and set a time to present your ideas. You have taken all the proper steps to get yourself to this point. You have a great understanding of the company and its needs, you have built relationships with multiple people in the organization, and you have a truly relevant idea for the organization you are trying to do business with. These steps have brought you closer to the close, and, unlike the jokers who send out blind proposals to any random company, you have high odds for closing this business. That doesn't mean you should ease up and get overly confident, though; you still need to close the business, and the presentation can be a make-or-break point. Make sure you are thoughtful in your approach in accomplishing this step.

★ **Create great presentations.** Use your industry standard as a guide. If most people in your industry use only a brochure, generate a dynamic slide show. If most people use slide shows, develop an interactive media presentation. Whatever it is you think your presentation needs, take it to the next level.

★ **Put together mockups that feel real.** Bring samples. Have these materials professionally created or rendered so your client sees a polished example of what you plan to offer.

★ **Anticipate the questions that will be asked.** Don't be caught off guard.

★ **Practice, practice, practice.** "Winging it" won't make you feel fresh; it only makes you look unprepared.

Through the entire new business funnel and up until this point, it has been all about the potential client. Now it's all about you and how well you represent and explain your concept and the level of effectiveness it will yield for the client. This is also the time to show the client how well you will look out for it and help it do business. You need to be buttoned up in all areas, from a killer presentation to a sharp suit. Every detail has to be addressed. Everything about the way you present yourself has to build the prospect's confidence. Your own confidence in your concept is crucial to closing business. If the client leaves the meeting with the confidence that you will deliver because he knows you're confident in yourself, you will close business.

The work you put into the presentation is crucial. Make sure you cover all the points that will help you build your case for the company doing business with you. Make sure your presentation is compiled with care and precision. And by all means, practice until the words that flow out of your mouth and all the concepts are as smooth and natural as breathing. Don't just make it look great; make sure you have a command of the material.

When I was in seventh grade, there was a science fair, and while I was deciding what my project would be about, my dad offered me a suggestion. He was a pharmacist, and he worked for a pharmaceutical company that had created great imagery on the human body. He had a bunch of medical books at the house, so assembling a well-thought-out, great-looking project was well within my reach. I spent my weekends for the next month carefully cutting images from the brochures, defining the parts, and making the project look awesome. I put a ton of work into my exhibit, and when the day of the fair arrived, I scanned the room, and no project rivaled mine. My confidence was high that I was taking home first place. The judges walked around the room, and as they did, they asked questions about the topics presented. They came to me and they had smiles, because they could see the work I'd put into it. Then they asked me two questions, and I fumbled and couldn't answer either. As hard as I had worked and as much effort as I had put into the project, I wasn't completely prepared, and I did not have a command of the material.

I came in second place. Second means first loser. Second means you are not getting the deal and some other company is. Do not let your work go for naught: prepare, practice, and anticipate the questions that will be asked.

It's more than 30 years later, and the funny thing is, I still remember one of the questions I was asked: "What is the size of your heart?" If I had known it was the size of my fist, I might be a doctor today. I know I am beating a dead horse, but I cannot stress enough how important preparation and practice are at this step of the process. They will be the difference makers in generating revenue. However, if you find yourself in a presentation and you do not know the answer to a question, make sure that you are honest at all times. *Never* make things up as you are going along. This is where salespeople get in trouble promising things that they can't deliver. Overpromising or misinformation at this stage will lead to issues later in the process. Don't do it.

One final thought: when you are creating a package and presentation for a potential client, keep a little something in your back pocket. What I mean is that you should deliberately not include everything possible in the package. Leave some inventory or services that you could deliver out of the presentation. It's just the nature of the beast for a potential client to ask for more, and naturally you will want to satisfy her requests and have something ready to be included, especially if she pushes hard and wants more. At this stage, you should leave out something that isn't at the core of what the deal is all about but that will please the client when she asks for more—and if, by some chance, she does not ask for more, later on down the line you can add it in anyway because that will make her feel like you are overdelivering, which you technically will be. That move will further strengthen the relationship. Either way, you'll be covered, and that is the objective of this step: to be fully prepared for whatever objection the prospect throws at you.

8. Exchange Ideas to Get to the Close

The reality is, no matter how prepared you are or how great a package you create, the potential client is going to want to put his stamp on the deal and make tweaks. If he wants to make wholesale changes, you obviously were not listening (or worse: he's crazy). But that aside, there most likely will be an exchange of ideas to get your prospect to a final comfort level with the deal and the confidence that it makes sense for his business. This give and take will provide the ammo for you to win the business. It may not always be necessary, but plan on it as a step that gives your client the sense that he has fine-tuned the deal so that you can get to the close.

This is a point where frustration can set in; it's easy to get agitated with the process. Don't give in and view this as just a final step to the client's verbal agreement and a contract. At times this exchange will also produce creativity and bring something fresh and inventive to the deal that makes it even better for both parties. Remember that the more deeply invested your prospect is in the details of the deal, the more likely it is that this will be the beginning of a long and mutually beneficial relationship.

9. Close/Dead

Once you have been true to the previous eight steps, you can then ask for the deal and go to contract. If you have been diligent in all these steps, you are most likely getting a verbal agreement. Because you have created a carefully crafted and specifically defined solution, the close will be much easier; deals at this level are never shots in the dark. The likelihood is that if the deal were going to be killed, it would have been nixed at a previous stage in the funnel. It can happen—and we'll look at some of those instances in the next chapter.

All this being said, it's important to remember that you have not technically closed the business upon receipt of the verbal "yes"; the deal is not done until you have a signed contract, so you have to make sure you are paying attention to the lawyers and how and why the contract is adjusted. Some lawyers have a knack for mucking up a business deal. You need to stay in control of the process and make sure the lawyers do not nose their way into the business points of a deal. Yes, they need to protect you and your potential partner, but they shouldn't be an impediment to business.

With almost every contract I have sent to clients, whether in radio, in TV, at the Patriots, or now at TrinityOne, I have seen lawyers attempt to make changes to the business deal. The funny thing is that it doesn't matter if it's a 10-page deal for 50 grand or an 80-page deal for millions—there always seem to be unnecessary changes to the deal points. A deal I did just a couple of years ago sticks in my mind vividly because of this phenomenon. The corporate lawyer for the company was hell-bent on telling me what our role was with her company. She even said to me, "I have been in this business 25 years, and I never have seen an alliance in which we didn't control that aspect of the business." I chuckle now because she actually believed she understood the sports marketing business better than her colleagues who had agreed to the deal and I did. When that sort of thinking crops up, that's when I end the call and circle back with the businesspeople, because the deal point was a business decision, not a legal one. You should do the same and not get into a jousting match with the lawyers. If something like this happens, they are just out to prove their value to their clients and do not care what is best for the relationship.

If you are going to get to a closed deal, you have to stay on the process after the verbal agreement and make sure you get a signature. Then—and only then—can you confidently declare that the deal is closed and that you're bringing revenue into your organization. There is no better feeling in business than closing new deals. It is always worth the effort and the process.

Whenever I introduce the nine steps of the new business funnel to a new salesperson, she invariably starts finding stronger, more viable prospects and begins building and caring for relationships with them that can lead to the sort of discovery and deal development we talked about. If you are disciplined in this process, your close rate will increase, and your relationship-building efforts will become far more fruitful and long-standing. Of course, as in everything, you'll come across some exceptions—the process won't take you where you would like to be, or you'll come across what amounts to just bad businesspeople—and even when you have a signed contract, you can expect that some people will not keep their word. Don't focus on the exceptions. Stick to the game plan, and you will generate revenue.

CREATING AND GENERATING

I would be remiss if I didn't wrap up this chapter by discussing the different skill sets of those who are gifted at developing creative solutions for other businesses and those who close deals. The key to the revenue game is the ability to do both. Marketers are charged with building relationships to generate revenue; however, the talent it takes to create pertinent programs and then sell them to a potential client typically doesn't emanate from one person. Don't fear collaboration; avoiding using the skills of everyone on your team isn't worth the lost revenue opportunity.

If you can create or sell, there is a place for you in the new business process. If by chance you have the talent to both create and sell, not only will you excel, but you will also find yourself charged with running the business. Those are the characteristics of the best CMOs.

DON'T SPIKE THE BALL
ON THE FIVE-YARD LINE

Now that you have the road map to revenue, you'll want to steer clear of some wrong turns that are easy to take once you're on the road—even with good directions. None of what we've talked about so far is brain surgery; if it were, I wouldn't be the one giving the advice. We've continually reinforced the discipline required for generating incredible revenue because we've seen so many deals and relationships crumble down the line. It's not always easy to follow through, so in this chapter, we're going to help you refine your focus so that you can cash in for yourself and your organization.

Every Sunday in the fall across the United States, football teams take to the field with two goals in mind: to score touchdowns and to prevent the opposition from doing the same. Imagine if, during the drive down the field, there was a breakaway play and one of the players found an open lane that would let him soar into the end zone. He wouldn't stop at the five-yard line and spike the ball. That would be absurd. Can you imagine the ridicule he'd face on ESPN? The network would replay the clip over and over. No player spikes the ball before the goal line; if he has a clear shot, he runs straight into the end zone and scores a touchdown.

Never in a million years would we expect to see a pro athlete give up on a play five yards shy of the end zone, so why are businesses and sales executives consistently willing to come up short? Everyone loves to jump the gun and cut corners, and it's this practice specifically that leads individuals to fall short of achieving their goals and never fully complete what they set out to accomplish. There are so many people with good intentions, but there are so few who have the discipline and the desire to execute the goals they set for themselves. This drive and discipline are what separate the exceptional people and companies from the mediocre ones. It doesn't matter how much talent someone has. If he doesn't follow through, the likelihood is that he will fall short of his goals and ultimately fail.

THE FIVE FACTORS OF DRIVE

In the next section, we've outlined the five primary elements of the successful business—and the businessperson—that continually reaches its goals. Conveniently, we call these elements the Five Factors of Drive. We hope you'll use these thoughts to help you ensure that you'll follow through and score.

Direction

First and foremost, you must have and work from a carefully developed plan that outlines *specific* goals. These goals could include a certain revenue number you'd like to hit or a particular client you'd like to land. The plan should include the details of what needs to be *done* (not what you hope will happen) to accomplish the desired outcome. Too many people embark on a mission with no forethought regarding what it will take to achieve their objectives. They often don't think ahead of time about what actions will aid them or, even more important, what might prevent them from reaching their goals. Before you begin any journey, make sure you have mapped out a route and have equipped yourself with the tools necessary for achieving your desired results. It seems obvious, but a clearly defined direction keeps you focused on exactly where it is you need to go.

Desire

Once a plan is in place and, again, before you set out on your mission, you must have the desire to truly want to do everything necessary to bring your vision to life. You may have the best business plan in the world, but if you aren't deeply invested in it personally, rest assured that you won't fulfill it. Keep in mind that you'll have to maintain this level of desire throughout the entire journey. Halfhearted efforts usually get derailed, so be sure you have a real passion for whatever it is you set out to accomplish. Once you feel that you have it in you to get it done, desire will carry you along the way and foster your follow-through. Desire is the foundation for all the other emotions that will come into play along the way. Make sure your desire is solid like a rock—before you rock.

Discipline

Here's where the rubber meets the road. You must follow the plan you have laid out. You must stay the course, and even when you don't feel motivated, you must have the discipline to complete the list of actions that will drive you to your objective. Do not let laziness deter you from moving toward your destination. Those who lack discipline will always waver and let failure creep in. Think about something as simple as working out: how awesome is the feeling you get when you hit the gym every day and stick to your regimen? Then one day you're not in the mood, one day becomes two, and the next thing you know, you're on the couch eating chips and dip. Anything you set out to do will be derailed without discipline. In fact, it's safe to say that discipline is the key ingredient of all the principles that contribute to winning the customer. Your sense of discipline will separate you from the rest of the pack; don't take it for granted.

Determination

There are going to be bumps in the road. Count on them. Whether you give in to roadblocks or stay the course reflects your determination and will resonate with your clients and customers. You must stay true to your mission, pushing past pitfalls and obstacles, and never allowing them to get the better of you. At times you may need to make adjustments to your plan—or pivot entirely—but don't let the details derail you from completing it. When you come to a hurdle, stop and assess the situation, and then make a decision about how to proceed. Taking a moment and avoiding reactionary decision making will help you reset your direction instead of running off the road.

Destination

After all your hard work and focus, make sure that the final product reaches the pinnacle of its realization. Don't cut corners just to say that you finished—your customers and clients will know. It's your job as an exceptional businessperson to be exceptional, and that means ensuring that you've done everything possible to complete the process and reach your ultimate goal to the absolute fullest. Reaching the destination that you designed in the first place will separate you from the norm; most people are satisfied with simple completion and are content with satisfactory, instead of exceptional, results. When we talked about the new business funnel, we reinforced that a deal is not closed until you receive a fully executed and signed contract. Be sure that you pay attention to every last detail—whether it is of a deal, a design, a memorable moment, or a promotion—so that you reliably achieve your goal. Don't spike the ball just before the goal line.

No matter what you may have heard about the benefits of cranking out work, you must know that the top executives at the most powerful companies across industries are performing with the five factors in mind. Their commitment has brought them high-level success—and it's because others took notice of their talents and abilities. The beautiful thing is that you have the choice to think and behave this way. The five Ds will compel you to do what you say you are going to do and help prevent you from being thrown off course.

Essentially, the five factors prevent you from throwing your hands in the air and giving up. That's the course many people take—and it's a course that leads to failure. You'll only truly fail when you stop trying.

SOMETIMES YOU JUST HAVE TO SUCK IT UP

When I was growing up, I lived in a three-decker tenement building in East Boston. I lived on the third floor with my mom and sister, and my grandparents lived on the first floor. Because of this arrangement, I spent a lot of time with my grandparents and learned their perspectives on what was truly important in life. Many of their ideas have stuck with me to this day, but one conversation in particular, a conversation that I had with my grandmother, probably set my life's course in motion.

My grandmother, Sarah, was a seamstress who sewed piecework for a clothing manufacturer in Boston. She took the train from East Boston to get to work every morning, as did I to get to Boston College High School.

Every morning we walked to the station and rode together up until her stop; then I continued on to Dorchester. Those shared morning commutes, while only in half-hour chunks, were a great bonding period for us.

I had made the decision (or should I say that I was led to *believe* that I had made the decision) to take the road less traveled and attend BC High. Most of my friends from grammar school stayed close by and went to high school in either East Boston or the North End; both were predominantly Italian and very safe, comfortable choices. BC High was an enormous leap for me, educationally, culturally, and personally. It wasn't that I lacked confidence at the outset; I just don't think I was equipped for my new circumstances. I had no friends, I was ill prepared, and culturally, I was at a loss.

Needless to say, my first three months at BC High were grueling. Whether it was because it was too difficult, it was too drastic a change, or just that too many new things were thrown at me at once, I spent many nights crying myself to sleep and questioning whether I had made the right choice. My parents discussed the possibility of my switching schools and wondered aloud if they had expected too much of me.

My grandparents knew all of the issues. We were a tightly knit family, and we talked about everything. The general consensus was, "Why are we putting Louis through this? He is so unhappy." No one wanted me to quit, but no one wanted me to crack, either. "Was it too much of a stretch for the boy?"

One morning, while my grandmother and I were walking to the train station, she turned to me and said, "You know, nobody will fault you for leaving." Then she paused, looked at me, and said, "Of course, except *you*. If you quit, you'll probably regret it for the rest of your life. Every excuse you give me to leave will be justified, but sometimes in life, you just have to suck it up, roll up your sleeves, and get it done. I know this is not what you want to hear from me. Whatever you decide to do, I will support you, but don't make the mistake I made." She herself had dropped out of school in the seventh grade. "You have to complete what you set out to do. You quit now, and the next time it will be easier . . . and the next, until you are 70 years old wondering why you quit everything in your life. That's all I have to say."

Character is not something that is taught in school. My grandmother knew what character was, and knew that if I quit, I didn't have any. So, suck it up I did. I was at a true crossroads in my life, and I was fortunate enough to receive proper direction and support from my family. It was a game changer and a lesson learned. From that day forth, I became unstoppable.

My grandmother passed away a few years ago, but her words echo in my head even more clearly today than when she spoke them to that 14-year-old boy. "You just have to suck it up, roll up your sleeves, and get it done."

GIVING UP IS NOT PART OF THE PLAN

Quite often, people create a project or set out on a particular road, only to quickly find themselves lost in visions of grandeur, excited about the prospect of succeeding or having a windfall. Then, as it always does, the unexpected happens: something pops up that becomes an impediment to that hoped-for success. I say "the unexpected happens," but realistically, roadblocks and pitfalls should be very much expected. It's very rare for a plan to be executed without a hitch. Maybe you're working on a deal, only to discover that your information is old and the company you are trying to bring into the fold has changed strategies. The unexpected could be as simple as a minor miscommunication.

Encountering an impediment to progress, no matter how legitimate it may be, provides a clear indicator of what you're made of, and how you handle it defines your character. You can boil reactions to setbacks down to three basic responses.

Quit

It's as simple as that: some folks can't face adversity and panic when it arises, so they pack up their toys and go home. When I was in radio working as an executive producer, a young man interviewed with me and expressed how much he loved sports and broadcasting and how he really wanted to break into the business and just needed someone to take a chance on him. His passion was obvious, but I was still a little guarded, because being a fan of the business and being a fan of sports are two very different things. I wasn't certain what really fueled his passion and what appeared to be his significant drive. There's a perfect job position in radio for testing this type of person's mettle: part-time, weekend overnights. It's brutal, and it's just what it sounds like—minimum wage, 11 p.m. to 7 a.m. Fridays, Saturdays, and Sundays. Whoopee!

He was solid for a full three months, and when a midday producer moved on, I moved the full-time overnight person to the midday producing slot. I offered the gung ho weekend producer the newly available full-time overnight gig and told him that if he was patient, he was next in line for a daytime slot. Another three months went by, and Mr. Gung Ho couldn't take it any more and resigned.

Two months after he left, the 1 p.m. to 9 p.m. slot opened up. If he had only stuck it out, just eight months after getting hired, he would have had a prime slot and could have been a program director for a sports radio station—or even been on the air. Last I heard, he was working in accounts receivable for some company outside of the sports industry, all because he gave up and showed little patience for the industry he supposedly loved. He might be in his dream job right now if he had shown some perseverance while working his way up.

But the fool quit.

Stay the Course

Some folks are completely focused on the mission in front of them and put their heads down during adversity to try to charge through the issues. This is admirable, and it doesn't always *sound* like an awful choice (in fact, it sounds pretty dedicated), but when the same course of action doesn't get you to where you need to be and your efforts become futile, it's probably best to change your direction and approach.

When I produced television shows back in the 1990s, I didn't actually work for the TV stations that aired our shows. I was a minority partner in a TV production company while I worked full-time in radio. We produced several shows and then negotiated deals with different stations to air particular programs. While we were negotiating, we typically dealt with the station's general manager; once the contract was signed, we worked with the station's production team to execute the delivery of the show. No matter what station we worked with, there always seemed to be tension between the station and our group. We were outsiders, and it appeared that this was just where the crews wanted us.

On one project, the person in charge of production appeared to seriously resent us, and this also carried over to his staff. Getting things done was always more difficult than it had to be. When we were producing the show, the staff members were constantly throwing up roadblocks to accomplishing even the simplest things. No matter how hard I tried or how much I worked to make their lives easier—no matter what I said or did—we were made to feel like intruders in their space.

Then, purely coincidentally, John Maguire, my GM at the radio station and one of my mentors in business, told me a story that struck a chord and was directly related to my situation. He'd recently read it in You^2 by Price Pritchett, which is a great read, and I'd highly recommend it. The story goes like this:

There was a man sitting on a porch in a rocking chair enjoying a breezy summer day. As he was gazing off into the distance, he noticed this little fly trying to leave the porch. The porch had a sliding glass door, and the fly was banging against the glass repeatedly—bang, bang, bang—trying to fly out of the porch. Obviously, the little fly saw the lake and the trees through the glass, but no matter how hard he tried, he could not escape. The man thought to himself that he had never seen anything with that much determination. That little fly was working harder than anyone the man knew, just to get out of the house. The ironic part of the story was that the sliding glass door was slightly open, and if that fly had just moved an inch to the left, he would have soared to freedom.

I instantly realized that I was that little fly, and I was approaching my situation with the station production crews completely wrong. Working hard, being organized, and having everything prepared were not going to change the way the crews viewed me personally, and that was always going to extend to our shows. I had to change my approach if I was going to change how we were perceived and treated. Just as that little fly needed to move a little to the left, I needed to shift my habits in order to stay on track with the station.

Even though I had to change the way I operated, I didn't have to change who I was. The next week, I walked into the TV station with some trays of Italian cold cuts and all the fixings. I was definitely greeted with a more positive response, but that was just the beginning. I took the time to learn about all the individuals on the team and made every effort to be engaging and thoughtful about their personal situations. Instead of being this outside producer who was all business, I opened up and invested in the group. Lo and behold, things began to run extremely smoothly, and we reached an enjoyable coexistence. I was no longer the outside guy.

John Maguire and Price Pritchett's story about the little fly made me realize that you have to be willing to remake the way you operate and be open to new methods to achieve your goals. There are many ways to reach your destination; you just need to choose the most efficient *and* the most enjoyable one. Everything in life, whether personal or business, is fluid; you can't be afraid of or resistant to adjusting to the circumstances and evolving with the times.

Adapt and Overcome

The folks who stop and think through multiple solutions are the most likely to achieve success. You can't let adversity stop you, but you have to be real about the situation and true to yourself. If your planned course is not the right one to achieve your goals, then you must alter the plan to get you to your destination. You should always approach your goals with focused flexibility: focused in that you know where you need to be, and flexible in terms of how you get there.

The first three months after I started my career in the NFL with the New England Patriots were pretty bumpy. Most of the folks at the team had been there for quite some time, even longer than the Krafts had been. To say that the people at the team operated with the "it's always been done this way" frame of mind would be a gross understatement. I had zero experience in the NFL, but it was clear to me that the way things were being done was extremely inefficient and that many great opportunities were being missed. Let's just say I wasn't making friends quickly at my new job.

It became quite frustrating because the organizational structure was much more linear than I was accustomed to at the radio station. Even though it was an NFL team, it was a family business (which, by the way, most teams are: billion-dollar family businesses, but family businesses just the same). At the time, Dan Kraft was my primary Kraft family contact. He had discovered me and brought me into the organization. Dan was great on two fronts: he was an unbelievable sounding board who was supportive and encouraging, but at the same time, he was not going to fix my concerns or problems. Initially, I didn't understand his actions, but I soon learned that his management was brilliant because it forced me to think differently and create my own solutions.

I played tug-of-war with many of the other departments and even with people within my own group. Folks were just complacent, happy to be there, and really uninterested in change or growth. However, I hadn't accepted the job just to sit back and take a paycheck; I wanted to make a difference and do great things for the owners. Being new to the organization was a hurdle, and pointing out that I had not worked for a team in the past was the "go to" response every time I suggested trying something new. "Lou, we can't do a draft party; no one is interested in that."

"If you had worked for a team before, you would know that" was one of my favorite responses—I heard it constantly. Funny enough, a draft party turned out to be the very event that launched my career with the team.

There was an old harness racetrack on the stadium grounds that the Krafts had just acquired. One day, I walked through the area and realized that the space was perfect for a video or TV event. There were hundreds of TVs wired all around the track because of the nature of racing, and telecasting the draft made perfect sense to me. The real beginning of the season was the NFL draft, not training camp, which was how some employees at the team saw it. The Krafts had hired me to run marketing, but what they really wanted me to do was create events that would drive traffic and generate revenue. This was right where they wanted me to be. I drew up a plan describing the event, the strategy, the upside, the downside, how to promote it, sponsorship opportunities, and selling tickets to the event; I gave them a full-throttle event plan.

Well, let's just say that the thought of this event didn't sit well with the longtime employees; the naysayers were everywhere—and they were vocal! But the only thing that mattered was that the Krafts thought it was a viable idea, and they gave me the go-ahead to prove what I was made of. There were people at the stadium who hoped the event would fail, so I received limited cooperation. But I was focused, and I had a small group of loyal people who jumped on board with me, in addition to some killer interns. We were rolling up our sleeves, moving tables, driving forklifts, and doing anything and everything we could to make this event successful, regardless of the support (or lack thereof) from other departments.

The event ended up being a huge success. The building was completely jammed with fans who were spending money and having a fun time being around the stadium and their team. I wasn't sure if other teams did this type of event (although many do now) because I was just focused on pulling this one off. In hindsight, it might have been smart of me to check out the other teams around the league. But I was determined to be a trendsetter, and quite frankly, I didn't care what other teams were doing. That attitude was the result of my inexperience, but it also fueled me, so no regrets.

After the event, I was driving home from the stadium, exhausted but satisfied, and I decided to check my messages. There were quite a few, but the one that stood out was from Dan Kraft. I could hear the satisfaction in his voice as he stated, "This is exactly what we hired you for. That was a great event; nice job." After that there really was no looking back. The naysayers were afraid to challenge me, and slowly, many of them either migrated my way or left the organization. The events and programs we created allowed for great revenue-generating mechanisms that were spectacular opportunities to engage and interact with our fans.

The key to all of this is that I believed in my ability, thought differently, and did not succumb to the mentality of "this is how it has always been done." Also, I can't fail to mention that the Krafts' leadership style allowed me to flourish. So, when people tell you, "It can't be done," or "It's always been done this way," don't subscribe to their myopic views. If someone does say this to you, then it's probably a great indication that it's time for a change. Always been done this way? I don't think so.

The fact of the matter is that the biggest obstacle to success is the person herself. Failure occurs when someone shuts down or is married to a plan of action. No goal is too lofty. Any goal is attainable. People are achieving their goals every day. What separates success from failure is what's inside the person making the attempt. If you are to reach your goals, you can never, ever give up, and you can't be obstinate about how you are going to get there. If you have the determination and the vision, you will achieve your goals. Don't give failure the satisfaction—never give up.

So, you have the personal makeup to see things through to the end, and you're bringing in clients and generating revenue for your organization. But, because you are a great Relationship Architect and you love to win over the customer, you may have a difficult time saying no to people. You can do everything correctly and show all the discipline and drive in the world, but if you can't say no, you'll end up dead in the water.

DON'T BE A DOORMAT

One major pitfall of building relationships is accidentally cultivating the inability to say no. It is a common misconception that the word *no* is purely a negative word or that it embodies a negative attitude. Although "no" is a negative response, which most of us do not want to hear, it reflects far more *reality* than "yes" might—and you need to view it that way, especially when you are the person using it.

Most people believe that great relationships are built on always saying yes to the other person. That is so untrue. When you are communicating within the boundaries of a solid relationship, the *truth* carries much more weight and creates a much stronger bond than simply a positive response. Unfortunately, delivering a positive is so much more fun. However, the problem remains that the aftermath will not be that much fun if that "yes" you just gave away is unobtainable. In personal relationships, you may receive a little flak when you fail to deliver on a promise, but in business, that failure is deadly and is typically "one and done" (unless there is a very long history of good experiences).

That being said, it's important to figure out how to break through the barriers and realize that "no" in a business relationship is not a bad thing if it is done at the appropriate time and for the appropriate reasons. Let's switch gears for a minute. I imagine that at some point in his or her life, everyone has had a girlfriend or boyfriend who was too available, who would always say yes too readily. If you haven't been in this situation yourself, you probably know someone who has been. Think about what that ease of access invokes. I can recall a number of situations where I have witnessed this behavior, and, invariably, the person who says yes all the time is taken for granted and is not truly respected—the person who is supposed to be generous becomes a virtual doormat and is walked all over. This is not a relationship anyone should want to be in, and it is certainly not what embodies the power of Relationship Architecture. In fact, this dynamic is absolutely destructive in any relationship and is sure to be an impediment to generating revenue—which, of course, is counterproductive to the entire reason why you have set out to do business.

You have not built a solid, mutually beneficial relationship if all you do is say yes. The reality is that "yes" is not always possible. I've had salespeople work for me throughout my career, and they generally have had an extremely difficult time with this concept because they tie the fear of saying no to their compensation. Salespeople typically believe they can't say no to a customer or a client for fear of losing revenue.

"No" does not have to mean a loss of revenue if the situation is handled properly.

I always stressed to my sales group that a thoughtfully delivered answer has much more impact than a rushed "yes." You must be absolutely sure that you can deliver before you offer the positive response. In this regard, "no" can be your friend and will earn you respect if you use it appropriately. Here are three ways to recognize when "no" is appropriate in a business relationship and when "yes" will drastically erode the relationship and prevent revenue.

1. You must say no when you know that the request is impossible to accomplish and that there is no chance of your delivering on the

agreement without the presence of luck. This also includes promises that could possibly be fulfilled, but would be so costly that they would exceed realistic expectations and go beyond what the relationship demands.

2. You must say no when the person making the request has continually asked for favors, perks, and additional items that are outside the scope of your relationship, without regard to the quantity of requests and with the deliberate intention of receiving more than she is giving. This one-sided situation is a clear indication that you are being taken advantage of.

3. You must say no when you are asked to do something unethical, immoral, or damaging to your reputation and the equity that you have built in your brand—personal or corporate.

Saying no in these situations should not damage the business relationship you possess with anyone: partner, client, or consumer. If saying no in these circumstances damages your relationship, then the relationship wasn't built properly in the first place. The most solid relationships exist when everyone participates to achieve a mutually beneficial result. Don't be afraid to be real. Don't be a doormat. Just say no!

That being said, you may still wrestle with saying no to existing clients. That's just reality; at times, once you have the business agreement and the revenue stream, you will encounter clients who are plainly difficult to deal with. Sometimes, as with family, you can't choose your clients. The revenue they generate is too attractive for the organization, so you have to put up with demands and attitudes that make your job difficult.

When the Patriots were still playing in Foxboro Stadium, we had to create opportunities outside of the building in order to generate revenue. We didn't have the Fidelity Investments Clubhouse as we did in Gillette Stadium, so we had to create makeshift hospitality for more of a VIP experience. Since we couldn't do much inside the stadium, we would put up tents in the parking lots and decorate them, heat them, and serve some very good food prior to the games. These tents also provided great places to hang after the game to avoid the horrendous traffic jam getting out of the stadium. The tents came with different bells and whistles and amenities—we called them the Kickoff Club and the Playoff Club. At one point, we were able to name the clubs because it made sense for liquor companies to associate their brand with our hospitality; Johnnie Walker became the title sponsor for the Kickoff Club. We cultivated solid relationships with the liquor companies that distributed beer and liquor, and our little makeshift hospitality options actually became quite successful and profitable. We worked with three major liquor companies, Schieffelin & Somerset, UDV, and Guinness/Diageo, each of which was home to multiple brands. We enjoyed great relationships with the executives at each company. They understood our need to work with many different groups, but of course each of them always tried to position its brands in better ways than the others, which was their job.

In the late 1990s, Diageo merged with UDV and Schieffelin & Somerset, which changed things significantly for us. The good news is that we were performing at a high level for all three companies, and they each had enjoyed the relationship with the Patriots and the results we were able to offer. Their individual track records led us to a seven-figure deal with Diageo that brought more revenue to the stadium than the three individual deals combined had. We at the team were all thrilled because the revenue grew, and we now could work synergistically with one group—which we all thought would make growing the relationship that much easier.

As it turned out, *thought* was the operative word. Because Diageo was in transition, each of the original groups remained in charge of its own brands, and as the dust settled on the new company, each group was jockeying for its strategic position and the success of its respective brands. We thought the timing was perfect because we were entering the new stadium, but because of the newness of the merger, we couldn't have been more wrong. These three great clients turned into a three-headed monster. We used to joke that the three groups, each of which had spent in the low six figures in the past, suddenly seemed to think that they had spent seven figures each. They became a bear of a company to work with, and the variety of personalities and decision makers magnified the issues and the demands. It became very counterproductive to our doing business, and we eventually parted ways. It was a large loss of revenue, but it had become impossible to manage, and it had become so troubling that it was affecting our performance in other areas. Cutting ties was the only fix. The sad part was that individually the three companies had been great clients, but together they were impossible.

Sometimes relationships in business, despite the revenue they bring, have to be terminated for the greater good of the company and your employees. There will be short-term pain, but in the long term, you'll find it's the best course of action.

In the Diageo case, the need to separate came as an extreme surprise, and the conditions of the merger really were the cause. All of the people with whom we had built relationships over that time were great to work with; the circumstances caused the negative result, and we never saw it coming.

This isn't always the case; there are people you are going to deal with in business who are just not good people. There are lazy, deceitful takers out there, and if you're not careful, they will happily suck the life out of you. You can't always choose the perfect client or business relationship, but there is no reason why you can't identify who they are and be prepared for their shenanigans. Being prepared always helps ease the pain.

WHEN THE DUST SETTLES: THE TASMANIAN DEVIL EFFECT

There are many pretenders out there, people who lack the character or the discipline to follow through on what they say they are going to do. At times we get caught up in their flair and flamboyance, which become a smoke screen that hides what they are truly about. I like to refer to this as the Tasmanian Devil effect, after the Warner Bros. cartoon character that appears in *Looney Tunes* segments. I like to refer to it this way because Taz spins so fast, creating a tornadolike cloud of dust that shimmers and catches your attention as he whizzes by, but when he stops and the dust settles, you realize it's just a single-minded creature with selfish intentions.

In a world that's so full of posturing, it can be difficult to identify a Tasmanian Devil, and you could get sucked into his vortex. Creating relationships with people who are inauthentic or potentially dishonest will never yield the revenue you're after because the money and the relationship potential aren't there in the first place. It's always better to pick out a Taz type before you get involved with him. Here are a few tips to help you recognize the pretenders among us.

1. A Tasmanian Devil always nods his head and says yes to everything you say. I don't care how brilliant you are; there must be something he disagrees with. If he only says yes, he's playing you and trying to reel you into believing he is loyal. Another telltale sign is his laughter at every one of your so-called witty comments. Sorry, but unless your name is Steve Martin, you're not that funny.

2. A Tasmanian Devil tells you he can do anything—no matter what it is—and never once suggests that he may not be the ideal person for a particular assignment. This kind of yes-man behavior should make you suspicious. In and of itself, this is not an indicator of fraud, but it's definitely something to watch.

3. A Tasmanian Devil commits to doing something, but there are perpetual delays in completing the task or a noticeable lack of communication in the process. When someone is sincere, she will typically keep you informed of her progress. Also, not fully completing what she committed to doing is like spiking the ball at the five-yard line.

4. You may be dealing with a Tasmanian Devil the first time that someone says, "No problem; I'm on it right away," but does not come through. This should immediately raise a red flag. Of course, multiple infractions are a dead giveaway, but pay attention to what people say when they take on tasks and how they follow through. *That* is the key to identifying someone who is thin on substance.

5. Watch out when folks tell you one thing and do another. I'm not talking about blatant lying—those people are obviously ones you want to steer clear of. Tasmanian Devils can have more subtle nuances; I'm taking about behaviors that don't seem so bad in and

of themselves but are indicators of the type of person you are try-ing to avoid. This can include commitments to e-mail, call, or meet you somewhere and then not following through. People are busy and it happens, but watch out for trends. Also, pay attention to how someone handles this sort of transgression. How apologetic is he? How do you know?

6. You're definitely dealing with a Tasmanian Devil when you come across someone who exaggerates and stretches the truth, *especially* when it comes to making himself appear bigger and more con-nected than he actually is. This one is tough, because there are many egos out there, and "ego" doesn't necessarily equate to "pre-tender." But, just because someone reads an article or a book on a subject doesn't make him an expert. Don't be fooled by propa-ganda; focus on substance.

7. It's normal for a Tasmanian Devil to be disorganized and unfo-cused, and to appear to be constantly accepting more and more commitments. When someone has too many balls in the air, it's a good clue that she doesn't care if a few drop.

These are seven of the more glaring indications that you are experi-encing the Tasmanian Devil effect. None of these alone means anything, but if you start noticing a few of them strung together, then it may be time to put that relationship at arm's length. You do not want to invest too much of yourself before the dust settles and it's too late. If the rela-tionship is already producing revenue for your organization or has the potential to do so, you have some serious decisions to make. Whenever possible, choose to forgo the dough and live in a much better work envi-ronment, even though it will be with a little less cash.

It's easy to get sucked in sometimes. I admit that I have been duped on a few occasions. I've met people who appear to have substance and honor, only to learn as time goes by that it's all a façade to mask their hidden agendas or inadequacies. Don't beat yourself up for falling into the trap; it happens to the best of us. Instead, learn from the experience in two ways: first, note the traits of the pretenders; and second, make damn sure you are not one of them.

If you want to ensure that you're not pulling the wool over others' eyes (and, even more important, your own), do what you say you are going to do. That's pretty much it. If you tell someone you are going to do something, make sure you do it at all costs—time, effort, and money. Your word is your bond and should be more valuable and enforceable than any legal document. Of course, there are always ways to rationalize and wiggle your way out of your commitments—you can even get support from others to back up your excuses. Ultimately, though, the only one you'll be fooling is yourself. Don't. You want to be able to get up in the morning, look in the mirror, and like what you see. Hold yourself to a higher standard and do what you say you are going to do. Period.

THERE'S A PRICE FOR EVERYTHING

While I was growing up, I was very fortunate to have had a strong family presence in my life. There was always family around us, and plenty of wisdom and experience that came with it. One night at the dinner table, I proudly mentioned to my grandparents that I had taken a shortcut in finishing a project for school. I can't remember what the topic was, but I remember being so impressed with myself that I'd figured out how to get around doing all the work and still being able to say I'd gotten the task done. My grandfather, whom I called "Bumpy," cleared his throat, put down his fork, and looked at me with a slight expression of disapproval. He said, "Louis, let me tell you something that happened to me when I was a young man."

When my grandfather was younger, there wasn't a lot of steady work. He would show up at different locations to see if he could make a day's pay at construction sites, the shipyards, or other places where they hired casual help. One of his first stops was always the shipyard because new shipments were continually coming in to be unloaded off the boats and onto trucks. My Uncle Rico had permanent work there, and he would always try to get my grandfather on the job whenever he could. Sometimes he was successful, and other times it didn't work out so well. Regardless, my grandfather would always hustle to make a buck.

One day, my grandfather got on the job, and the crew was loading butter and other perishable supplies onto trucks. At one point toward the end of the shift, one of the cases of butter fell off the truck. It burst open, and it was customary at that time, because of the tight economic conditions, for workers to help themselves when that happened. My grandfather was a hardworking, honest guy, and he made a point of staying away from those situations, sticking to his job and minding his own business. My Uncle Rico was the eldest brother, and he had to take care of his brothers and sisters all of his life (my great-grandfather died when they were kids), so he looked at life differently and would not only partake, but also support the practice of encouraging parcels to "fall off the truck."

I want to clarify that my Uncle Rico had the best interests of his family in mind. He was saddled with the responsibility of fending for his family and, as an Italian immigrant, his circumstances were much different from what I, and most others, have ever experienced in our lifetimes. Nevertheless, Uncle Rico definitely cut corners and did some questionable things. I have to admit, it never altered my opinion of the man; I really loved him and enjoyed his company.

At any rate, on this particular night, my grandfather was punching out to head home when my Uncle Rico came over to say good night. When he hugged my grandfather, he shoved a box of butter into his coat. He told my grandfather to go home and bring it to his family. My grandfather was a nervous and conservative man normally, but walking home with the stolen butter in his coat, he was a nervous wreck. He explained to me how during the entire walk home, he was so worried about the wrong thing he was doing that he clutched the butter tighter and tighter.

When he finally got to the apartment, he was sweating and flushed. He opened his coat and handed my grandmother the butter, which was all melted and had turned to mush. He was so stressed out and had gripped the butter so tightly that he had rendered it useless.

He looked up at me after telling the story and said, "Louis, there is no such thing as cutting corners. Nothing is free. You will pay, one way or another. Work hard and earn what you get; it's far more satisfying." He then told me that he never took anything again in his life. He stuck to earning what he was able to, and, even though they may have had less, he was a happier man for it.

Because of my man Bumpy, I now realize that you are only fooling yourself when you cut corners in any aspect of life. You may get away with it in the short term, but it will always catch up with you. Put in the hard work up front, invest the appropriate time, and plan appropriately in advance; this approach will reliably serve you well. Cutting corners is sure to cause you grief and bring unhappiness. Nothing worth having comes easily, and nothing, *nothing* is for free.

All of the principles we've laid out in this book are out of respect for that basic premise: nothing great comes easily or accidentally. Anything worthwhile comes at some sort of price and, as the old Fram Oil Filter commercial always pointed out, "You can pay me now, or you can pay him later."

If you take nothing away but this, remember that an up-front investment of time, energy, and money is always less expensive in the long run than fixing poorly designed and developed decisions. Disorganized guesswork, going solely on your gut instincts, and operating your business by the seat of your pants will only lead to dissatisfaction and failure. Putting a great plan in place, designing an operational structure around it, and bringing it to life with great relationships is the only foolproof way to consistently win the customer and generate incredible revenue every time.

When I first started with the New England Patriots, one of the first things I worked on was an interactive fan event called Patriots Experience. I happened to meet with Mike Kellogg, my friend and a former colleague at the radio station, during the planning stages and told him about some of our plans and what we were working on. He stopped me and said (I'm paraphrasing, of course), "Lou, you are going to create so many things and have experiences that will culminate in 'The book of Lou.' You have to make sure you write everything down in a journal and document your experiences." He went on to reinforce that the details of everything I did would be valuable once I left the team.

I'd like to say this book came from the journal that Mike so wisely told me to keep, but I had to re-create and relive what happened in order to write it. I was fortunate that the memories and stories have largely stuck with me and propelled my philosophies, but I made a mistake when I didn't jump all over Mike's journal idea the second he headed out the door. Don't make the same mistake I made and procrastinate.

As with any endeavor, winning the customer doesn't happen overnight. We've given you insight into how to structure your organization, how to quickly build strong relationships that work for you, and how to design a new business funnel that equips you to consistently close new sales. The three work harmoniously together to ensure your strategic success. To get to that end, you have to get going.

So where do you begin?

Here's what you can do today to begin winning the customer and maximizing revenue. Ask the questions that will lead you to optimizing your organization and lead you to solutions:

★ **Take stock of your team.** How are you structured? Who does what job in your organization? Is there overlap? How can you begin to increase communication but separate responsibility? How can you optimize internal communication and communication with your customers? Do you have a database? Do you use it properly?

★ **Develop a relationship inventory.** What does your network look like? What do you know about the individuals you interact with? Who are your core customers? Do you have a system in place to continue building and gathering?

★ **Analyze your sales process.** Are you a transactional sales organization? What steps do you take when prospecting? How many meetings do you have before you ask for business? Are you building or selling?

These questions should help kick-start the process for you. Now's the time to get going: the ideas and philosophies are fresh in your memory, and you are excited about taking your organization to the next level. Once you've gotten started, you'll find it easy to gather momentum. If you're looking for inspiration, we're always adding new tools at www.louimbriano.com. Visit us there or contact us at lai@louimbriano.com.

Now go out and win the customer!

Lou Imbriano, the vice president and chief marketing officer of the New England Patriots football team from 1997 to 2006, is president and CEO of TrinityOne, a marketing company specializing in creating strategy for corporations to maximize revenue generation through building customer relationships and becoming custodians of the brand. Formerly a radio and television producer, he has appeared on numerous local Boston radio and television programs. Lou has been profiled on Forbes.com as one of the "Names You Need to Know" and has written multiple columns for the *Sports Business Journal*. Lou, who teaches sports marketing at Boston College, is based in Boston, Massachusetts.

Visit Lou at www.louimbriano.com.

Elizabeth King, a professional writer and test preparation educator, is author of *Outsmarting the SAT*. She lives in New York City.

CPSIA information can be obtained
at www.ICGtesting.com
Printed in the USA
BVHW041327180920
589115BV00009B/80

9 780071 775267